Do-It-Yourself

ALTO SAX

BY SAM FETTIG

PLAYBACK+
Speed • Pitch • Balance • Loop

To access audio and video visit:
www.halleonard.com/mylibrary

Enter Code
2175-4974-0622-1949

ISBN 978-1-5400-9755-2

Visit Hal Leonard Online at
www.halleonard.com

Contact us:
Hal Leonard
7777 West Bluemound Road
Milwaukee, WI 53213
Email: info@halleonard.com

In Europe, contact:
Hal Leonard Europe Limited
42 Wigmore Street
Marylebone, London, W1U 2RN
Email: info@halleonardeurope.com

In Australia, contact:
Hal Leonard Australia Pty. Ltd.
4 Lentara Court
Cheltenham, Victoria, 3192 Australia
Email: info@halleonard.com.au

CONTENTS

4 **INTRODUCTION**

5 **LESSON 1** Assembly and Maintenance

7 **LESSON 2** Tone Production

9 **LESSON 3** The Staff

12 **LESSON 4** Rhythm

15 **LESSON 5** First Notes

18 **LESSON 6** Technique Drills

22 **LESSON 7** Scales and Transpositions

24 **LESSON 8** Tempo and Style

34 **LESSON 9** Articulation

38 **LESSON 10** Road Maps

48 **LESSON 11** Syncopation

63 **LESSON 12** Eighth Rests and Sixteenth Notes

72 **LESSON 13** Intonation

78 **LESSON 14** Intervals

85 **LESSON 15** Cut Time

89 **LESSON 16** 6/8 Time

94 **LESSON 17** Chromatics and Enharmonics

97 **LESSON 18** Form

104 **LESSON 19** Other Keys

113 **LESSON 20** Improvisation

75 Legend Spotlight: Charlie Parker

115 Advanced Techniques

120 Sax Talk

127 Fingering Chart

SONG INDEX

53 Addams Family Theme
64 All About that Bass
65 All Star
33 America, the Beautiful
33 Anchors Aweigh
65 Another One Bites the Dust
70 The Banana Boat Song
37 Beauty and the Beast
49 Beer Barrel Polka (Roll Out the Barrel)
93 Believer
64 Blister in the Sun
40 Blowin' in the Wind
111 Can Can
49 Can You Feel the Love Tonight
103 Can't Buy Me Love
56 Can't Help Falling in Love
39 Can't Stop the Feeling!
68 The Candy Man
66 Centerfold
54 Chariots of Fire
44 Chim Chim Cher-ee
81 Cupid Shuffle
24 Danger Zone
37 Edelweiss
52 Eight Days a Week
30 Eine Kleine Nachtmusik ("Serenade")
96 Entry of the Gladiators
51 Every Breath You Take
82 Eye of the Tiger
69 Fly Me to the Moon (In Other Words)
59 Forever Young
41 Forrest Gump – Main Title (Feather Theme)
66 Funeral March
26 The Godfather (Love Theme)
28 Goin' Out of My Head
66 The Good, The Bad and the Ugly (Main Title)
49 Groovin'
95 Habanera
92 Hallelujah

80 Have I Told You Lately
84 Hey Ya!
29 Home on the Range
98 Hound Dog
25 Hush, Little Baby
45 I'm a Believer
91 I'm Popeye the Sailor Man
68 If You're Happy and You Know It
65 Iron Man
73 Isn't She Lovely
112 It's the Hard-Knock Life
27 Jupiter
47 Theme from "Jurassic Park"
55 Just My Imagination (Running Away with Me)
36 Karma Chameleon
32 Largo
39 Lean on Me
50 Livin' on a Prayer
30 London Bridge
43 Londonderry Air
25 The Longest Time
24 Love Me Tender
31 Lullaby
79 Mercy, Mercy, Mercy
101 Misty
36 Mony, Mony
42 Moon River
90 The Mulberry Bush
85 Musette
46 My Favorite Things
28 Na Na Hey Hey Kiss Him Goodbye
75 Now's the Time
30 Ode to Joy
50 Oh, Pretty Woman
50 Old Time Rock & Roll
100 Over the Rainbow
39 Oye Como Va
62 Piano Man
96 The Pink Panther
90 Pop Goes the Weasel
26 Rock and Roll All Nite
99 Rock Around the Clock

71 Rolling in the Deep
29 Rondeau
54 Seven Nation Army
28 She'll Be Coming 'Round the Mountain
110 Sherry
26 The Siamese Cat Song
88 (Sittin' On) The Dock of the Bay
64 Smoke on the Water
41 Some Day My Prince Will Come
53 Spongebob Squarepants Theme Song
74 Stand by Me
67 The Star-Spangled Banner
57 Summertime
86 Supercalifragilisticexpiali-docious
44 The Surprise Symphony
76 Sweet Caroline
25 Sweet Dreams Are Made of These
99 Sweet Home Chicago
31 Swing Low, Sweet Chariot
27 Symphony No. 1 in C Minor
57 Take Me Out to the Ball Game
58 That's Amoré (That's Love)
26 To a Wild Rose
66 To Be with You
98 The Twist
37 U Can't Touch This
65 Under Pressure
106 Uptown Girl
108 The Way You Look Tonight
36 We Are Family
91 We Are the Champions
102 What a Wonderful World
36 Whistle While You Work
60 Wonderful Tonight
83 Y.M.C.A.
77 Yesterday
87 You Can't Hurry Love

INTRODUCTION

Welcome to *Do It Yourself Alto Saxophone!* This book is designed for anyone learning to play for the first time. It will take you step by step from the very beginning. If you've never touched a saxophone and you can't read music, you can open this book and do it yourself. Just be sure to study in page order, as the material presented builds progressively.

You'll find over 120 songs that reinforce topics covered in twenty lessons. With styles ranging from classical to jazz, rock to rap, there are sure to be songs you'll enjoy. In addition to lessons and songs, there are "Toolboxes" throughout that introduce new concepts. Finally, you can dive deeper into the world of the alto saxophone by checking out "Advanced Techniques" and reading articles in the "Sax Talk" section.

On page 1, you will find a unique code. Go to **www.halleonard.com/mylibrary** and enter that code to give access to audio and video online, for download or streaming. There you will find expert video instruction to get you started on the right foot, plus video and audio demonstration of many songs found in this book. These spots are indicted throughout the book by these symbols:

Also included is PLAYBACK+, a multi-functional audio player that allows you to slow down audio without changing pitch, set loop points, and pan left or right—available exclusively from Hal Leonard.

It's worth noting that once you learn the alto saxophone, you'll have the skill and understanding to play any member of the saxophone family, whether tenor, baritone, or soprano saxophone. Learning to play the saxophone can be a fulfilling hobby or a serious pursuit. Either way, it is a highly rewarding experience. Whatever your goals, we hope you enjoy the journey and discover the fun of playing the saxophone.

LESSON 1:
Assembly and Maintenance

ASSEMBLE THE SAXOPHONE

1. Wet the reed while you assemble the saxophone by holding the thin end (tip) in your mouth. Be careful to not break the fragile tip.

2. Wear the neck strap around your neck and hook it into the ring on the back of the main body.

3. Insert the neckpiece into the opening at the top of the main body as follows:

   - With one hand, grasp the main body firmly but be sure not to bend any rods or keys.

   - With your other hand, insert the neck into the neck receiver (the opening). You may need to twist the neck back and forth as you insert it.

   - You may first need to loosen the neck receiver screw by hand.

   - Align the neck so that it does not angle away from the main body.

   - Retighten the neck receiver screw if necessary.

   - Adjust the neck strap so the cork on the neck is near your mouth when the saxophone is hanging. The exact neck strap adjustment will be addressed in Lesson 5.

With the saxophone hanging from the neck strap, your left hand will come around the top half of the saxophone and your fingers placed over those keys. Your right hand will come around the bottom half of the saxophone and your fingers placed over those keys.

This will allow you to keep the instrument steady for now. Exact placement of your thumb and fingers will be covered in Lesson 5. In fact, you will be setting the instrument aside (if standing) or across your lap (if sitting) for the next steps.

Assemble the Reed, Ligature 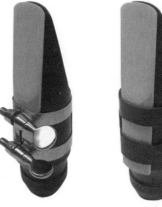 and Mouthpiece

For these steps, it is recommended that you lay the saxophone across your lap if you are seated or set it aside if standing.

1. Fasten the reed to the mouthpiece.

   - The ligature screw belongs on the right side of the mouthpiece. The two most common ligature designs are shown here.

   - The tip of the reed should be aligned with the tip of the mouthpiece.

   - The sides of the reed should be aligned with the edges of the mouthpiece.

2. The most important thing about reed placement is to ensure that air does not escape out the sides where the reed makes contact with the mouthpiece. This will be explained in further detail in troubleshooting section of the next lesson.

3. The second most important thing about reed placement is the position of the tip. Be sure it is even with the tip of the mouthpiece, as stated earlier. Exceptions to this are detailed in the Sax Talk article "Reeds" on page 121.

Maintenance and Storage

1. **DAILY**

   - Always store your reed in a reed case and never leave it on the mouthpiece. The individual plastic sleeve your reed likely came in is sufficient for now. Reed cases (preferred) can be purchased, and are discussed in further detail in the Sax Talk article "Reeds" on page 121.

   - Swab the main body when you are done playing. This prevents moisture from accumulating and damaging the pads. The following instructions are for a string swab with a cloth at one end and a small weight on the other end:

     › Remove the neck. Drop the small weight into the bell.

     › Turn the saxophone upside down so the weight drops out of the neck receiver.

     › Grab hold of the weighted end of the string and pull the swab all the way through.

     › Do this three times to ensure that no moisture is left inside the saxophone.

   - Apply cork grease to the neck cork weekly (rather than daily). A dry cork will eventually break off and need replacing.

2. **MONTHLY**

   - Clean the inside of the mouthpiece and neck with a cleaning brush. These are made specifically for this purpose and can be purchased. A small, hard-bristled toothbrush will also work.

   - The mouthpiece can be washed with soap and warm water. Do not bathe the neck in this manner because you do not want the cork to get wet.

   - Wipe the saxophone body with a soft cloth. Dust and lint can build up, especially in the small spaces between the rods and keys.

   - Adjustments and repairs are best left to a repair technician. But you can keep your eye out for screws that begin to back out. Tighten them with a small screwdriver as needed.

LESSON 2:
Tone Production

FORM AN EMBOUCHURE AND PLAY

Play this exercise with only the neck and mouthpiece (remove the neck from the body). You can let the saxophone hang if standing, rest on your lap if sitting, or set it down.

An **embouchure** is the way a musician applies the mouth to the mouthpiece. Follow the instructions here to establish a proper embouchure from the beginning. Keep in mind that your tone (sound) is a product of personal experimentation and adjustments which are addressed in the troubleshooting section on this page.

1. Cover your lower teeth with your lip and place your top teeth about a half of an inch from the tip of the mouthpiece.

2. Close your mouth securely around the mouthpiece but do not bite down. Both lips should be aligned together; your lower lip should not stick out.

3. Take a deep breath and play a long steady tone. With only the neck it will sound a bit comical, similar to a goose call.

TROUBLESHOOTING YOUR TONE

1. Reeds are finicky. They may play well one day and poorly the next. Choose a reed that is not chipped and has a straight tip (not warped). Avoid strong reeds early in your development (favor 2's and 2½'s over 3's and 3½'s). There is more information about reeds in the Sax Talk article on page 121.

2. Experiment with how much mouthpiece is in your mouth. Too much and it will honk wildly. Too little and you may not get a sound.

3. Make sure the reed is sealing at the sides. You should be able to create a vacuum effect against your hand by following these steps:

   • Place the mouthpiece receiver against the palm of your hand.

   • Form an embouchure and breathe in, causing the mouthpiece to form a suction against your hand before it "pops" away from the seal. If it does, you are in good shape. If the seal lasts for several seconds or longer, you are in great shape.

   • If the mouthpiece does not seal to your hand:

     › Remove the reed, wet it and clear any excess moisture. Then put it back on. It's similar to restarting your computer when something isn't going right.

     › If that doesn't work, find a reed that seals.

TONGUING

Tonguing is the proper way to start (or articulate) each note. Later you will learn when it's appropriate to play without tonguing, but tonguing is the default articulation.

Start each note by touching the tip of your tongue to a spot near the tip of the reed, then blow just as you would say "tah." The note is articulated when your tongue releases the air, much like a dam releases river water or your thumb releases water from the garden hose.

The following example has a few longer notes followed by some shorter notes. Feel free to play as many tongued notes as you want using whatever rhythm you want; experimentation is an important part of the learning process.

tah   tah   tah   tah   tah

LESSON 3:
The Staff

This lesson along with Lesson 4 is an overview of reading music. You are encouraged to reference these pages as you encounter the concepts throughout the book

Music is a language that you can read and write. Like any language, music has its own symbols and structure. You learned your native language because you were surrounded by it from birth. If you surround yourself with the language of music, you will become familiar with it over time.

THE STAFF

Music is organized on a staff of five horizontal lines. It is capable of displaying virtually all there is to know about a piece of music. Two important things it shows us is how music moves over space and time (rhythm) and how high or low the notes are (pitch).

Rhythm is organized horizontally along the staff and will be covered in the next lesson. Pitch is organized vertically using the lines and spaces; the higher a note's placement, the higher the pitch.

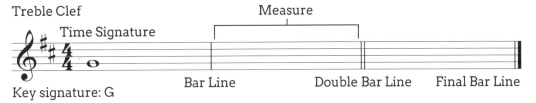

Treble Clef

The treble clef establishes the second line as the note G. The symbol itself is an ornate G, also known as a G Clef. Notice that it curls around the second line to establish G. There are other clefs, but the saxophone only reads in treble clef.

Bar Lines

Bar lines divide the staff into measures. A double bar line is used to mark something significant that occurs in the music, such as a new section. The final bar line is used to mark the end of the song.

Measures

A measure is the space between bar lines. It's also known as a "bar." The movement of music (rhythm) is established from left to right through this space.

Time Signature

The time signature determines how many beats are in each measure and what type of note receives one beat. This is covered in Lesson 4.

Key Signature

The key signature assigns either sharps or flats (never both together) for particular notes for the duration of the song. This is covered later in this lesson as well as in Lesson 7.

Spaces

Notes in the spaces in ascending order happen to spell the word FACE.

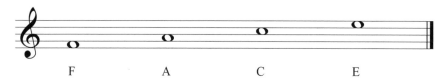

F   A   C   E

Lines

An acronym commonly used to remember notes on the lines in ascending order is Every Good Boy Does Fine.

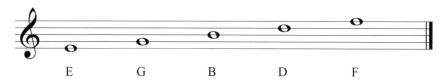

E   G   B   D   F

Alphabet

When the spaces and lines are combined, you'll see that music ascends alphabetically from A to G. You may find it helpful to memorize and locate A as you learn.

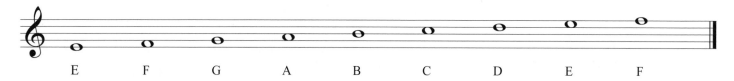

E F G A B C D E F

Ledger Lines

The staff can be thought of as an infinite number of lines; five of them are visible and the rest are invisible. When a note is needed above or below the staff, small lengths of line become visible. For instance, high B is in the space above the first ledger line. Low C is on the first ledger line below the staff.

Notice that this is a continuation of the alphabet.

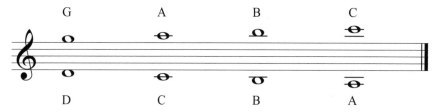

Accidentals

A half-step is the smallest interval (distance) between two notes. A note is altered by one half-step the following three ways:

 **FLAT**
Lowers a note
one half step

 **SHARP**
Raises a note
one half step

 **NATURAL**
Cancels a
sharp or flat

An accidental applies to a note for one measure. In this example the last note does not require a natural to cancel the flat; this is accomplished buy the key signature.

Sometimes you'll see a courtesy reminder in parenthesis. This example will sound the same as the previous example.

Here are two examples of accidentals in the context of a key signature. The key signature assigns sharps to all F's and C's. The natural symbol cancels each one until the next measure. Notice there is no courtesy reminder in the second measure.

LESSON 4:
Rhythm

TIME SIGNATURES

Rhythm is based on evenly spaced pulses that we call beats. The distribution of beats is determined by the time signature. The top number represents how many beats are in each measure, while the bottom number represents what kind of note receives one beat.

4/4
There are 4 beats per measure
A quarter note ♩ is one beat

6/8
There are 6 beats per measure
An eighth note ♪ is one beat

NOTE AND REST DURATIONS

The most common time signature is 4/4 time. The bottom number in 4/4 determines the following durations, whether sound (notes) or silence (rests):

WHOLE NOTE & REST
Each is four beats

HALF NOTE & REST
Each is two beats and
one half of a whole note

QUARTER NOTE & REST
Each is one beat and
one quarter of a whole note

EIGHTH NOTE & REST
Each is 1/2 beat and
one eighth of a whole note

SIXTEENTH NOTE & REST
Each is 1/4 beat and
one sixteenth of a whole note

BEAMS

Eighth notes and sixteenth notes are joined by horizontal beams, typically in groups of two and four. Eighth notes can be joined together with sixteenth notes, as you'll see in Lesson 12.

COUNTING METHOD

In this book, we will count rhythm using the method shown in the chart below. Note durations from the previous page have been placed into a table with sixteen columns. This table is always theoretically present in a musician's thinking when playing in 4/4 time. It represents all the ways notes and beats can be divided into smaller parts.

SUBDIVIDING

Subdivide notes in order to keep your place and play with rhythmic accuracy. This is done by thinking internally, tapping a foot, or using a metronome. You can do this right now: whistle, hum, or simply exhale while tapping your foot and counting in your head (stop on 5). You just performed a whole note.

Another example of subdividing that you can do right now: clap four quarter notes while counting eighth notes: "1-&-2-&-3-&-4-&" (& = and). You'll say a number on each clap with &'s between claps. We call the numbers downbeats, and the &'s upbeats.

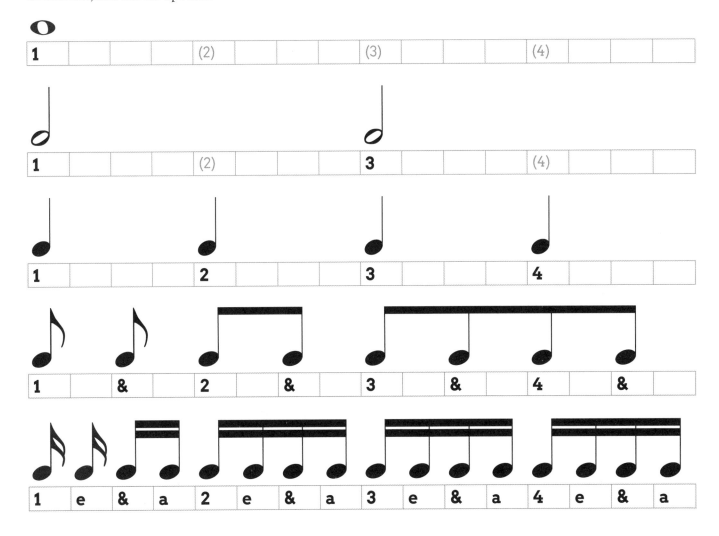

RESTS

Rests are counted and subdivided just like notes but are silent. Some rests are added here with the counting italicized in parentheses.

Try counting the half note in the second line like this: while clapping the downbeats, say a long "one" and stop on the third clap.

TIES

A tie is an arc that joins two notes of the same pitch together. In this example two quarter notes are tied and become a single note worth two beats. Ties are not to be confused with slurs which use the same symbol, but connects notes of different pitches. Slurs will be covered in Lesson 9.

ADDITION

As you saw with ties, rhythm involves a little math. Notice beat four of the sixteenth note line (bottom right of table). There is an eighth rest instead of two sixteenth rests because it is more efficient: 1/4 γ + 1/4 γ = 1/2 γ

Another bit of math we do involves dotted rhythms. This is covered in the Toolbox on page 29.

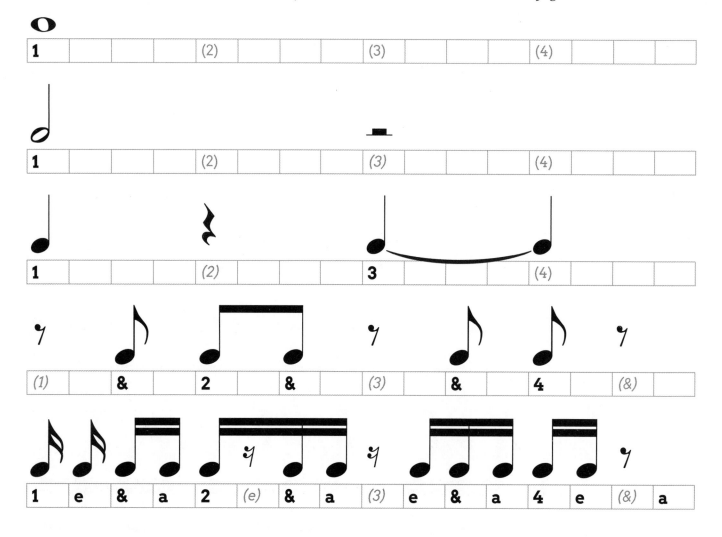

LESSON 5:
First Notes

GET IN PLAYING POSITION

1. Place your thumbs on the thumb rests as shown below.

2. Place the index (1), middle (2), and ring (3) fingers of each hand on the keys as labeled below.

3. Adjust the neck strap so you are looking straight ahead when the mouthpiece is in your mouth.

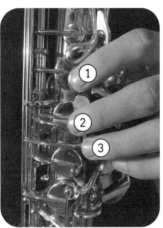

left hand   *right hand*   *right hand*   *left hand*

back view of saxophone   *front view of saxophone*

standing position

sitting position

LEARN YOUR FIRST NOTE

1. Long Tones

Take a deep breath and play an A for about 10 seconds. Pause to take another deep breath and repeat.

NEW NOTE: A

pause   *pause*   *etc.*

2. Octave Key

The octave key (left hand thumb) will raise the note one octave higher (8 notes apart). This works for many notes, but not all. Try it using the A you just learned.

NEW NOTE: HIGH A

add thumb

The line connecting the two notes is called a *slur*. This means you do not tongue the second note. Simply add the octave key while blowing.

3. Build to Five Notes

Now you will play some rhythms one line at a time starting with your first note A. The goal, in addition to learning new notes, is to become familiar with basic whole, half, quarter, and eighth note rhythms. Continually refer to the counting below each note as explained in Lesson 4.

Metronome

A metronome is a tool that provides an audible beat such as a click sound, and a visible beat such as a pulsing flash. and can be easily found as an application for your phone or other device. Practicing with a metronome is an excellent way to maintain rhythmic accuracy and develop a strong internal pulse. A metronome uses a measurement called beats-per-minute (BPM), often expressed as quarter notes per minute. Choose a comfortable BPM that allows you to play this page accurately. A recommended starting point is ♩=80.

NEW NOTE: A

1   3   1   2   3   1   1   2   &   3

NEW NOTE: B

1   2   3   4   &   1   3   1   2   3   1   &   2   3

NEW NOTE: G

1   2   &   3   4   1   2   3   1   2   &   3   4   1

1   3   4   &   1   2   3   1   4   1

NEW NOTE: C

1   3   1   2   3   1   &   2   3   &   4   1   &   2   3

1   &   2   &   3   &   4   1   &   2   &   3   &   4   1   &   3   &   2   &   3

NEW NOTE: D

1   3   1   2   3   1   2   3   4   1   3

All notes D and above will use the thumb key.

LESSON 6:
Technique Drills

These exercises will train your fingers to recognize and play notes. The muscle memory you develop will help you play the songs later in the book.

As in the previous page, remember to:

- Use a metronome.
- Take a deep breath before playing.
- Tongue each note.

NEW NOTE: ALTERNATE C*

*Use alternate C fingering when moving back and forth to B…

*Use alt. C here…   **…but not here because of the preceeding note.

Alt. C entire line

Alt. C this measure only

NEW NOTE: E

TOOLBOX

AIR

Because our default breath is quite shallow, we need to make a conscious effort to breathe deeply until it becomes a habit. Expand your belly and fill you lungs from the bottom. Do not raise your shoulders.

NEW NOTE: F

NEW NOTE: F#

*The sharp (#) will apply for the entire measure (see Lesson 3: Accidentals).

NEW NOTE: G   **NEW NOTE: A**   **NEW NOTE: B**   **NEW NOTE: C**

Add the octave key for the second note in each measure.

The octave key is down for this exercise.

*Alternate C fingering

This is Technique Drill 4 on page 18 with the octave key added.

*Alternate C fingering

NEW NOTE: F#   **NEW NOTE: F**   **NEW NOTE: E**   **NEW NOTE: D**

The octave key works the other way around. Learn new low notes using notes you already know. Remove the thumb for the second note in each measure.

NEW NOTE: B♭

LESSON 7:
Scales and Transpositions

SCALES

Scales are the building blocks of music much like the alphabet is for language. The major scale is the common starting point for musicians. While an experienced musician will know all twelve, songs in this book use only the five on this page (exception: Lesson 19: Other Keys).

KEY SIGNATURE

The key signature is found between the clef and time signature. It assigns a sharp or flat to a particular note for the entire piece of music. It eliminates the need to place a sharp or flat every time the note appears. This means a musician must be keenly aware of the key signature at all times.

TRANSPOSITION

The alto saxophone is a transposing instrument. This means you cannot play along with a different instrument while reading the same music. A piano is an example of a non-transposing instrument, also referred to as either a "C instrument" or a "concert-pitched" instrument. You would have to play an E♭ on the piano to match the C on your saxophone. This is why it is called an E♭ alto saxophone. Officially, the alto saxophone sounds a major sixth lower than written in concert pitch.

G MAJOR SCALE (CONCERT B♭)
There is an F♯ in this key signature.

C MAJOR SCALE (CONCERT E♭)
There are no sharps and no flats in this key signature.

F MAJOR SCALE (CONCERT A♭)
There is a B♭ in this key signature.

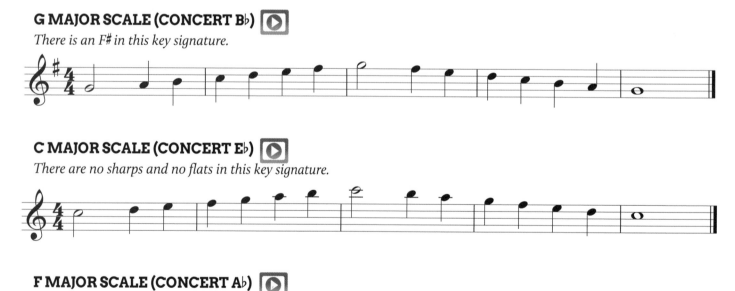

D MAJOR SCALE (CONCERT F)

There is an F# and a C# in this key signature.

NEW NOTE: C#

A MAJOR SCALE (CONCERT C)

There is an F#, a C# and a G# in this key signature.

NEW NOTE: G#

LESSON 8:
Tempo and Style

Tempo is the speed of music and style is the manner in which it is played. These are often indicated above the first measure. The style indication may be a genre such as rock or jazz. It may also be an adjective written in Italian such as dolce (sweetly).

Italian musicians in the 16th Century expanded music notation to include more detailed descriptions and instructions. The terms they used were fashionable throughout Europe at the time, and the Italian language has been the standard ever since.

While there are certainly English tempo markings like "fast" and "slowly," some of the common Italian terms listed here will be used throughout this book. Along with each term and definition is a measurement called beats per minute (BPM). This can be set on a metronome. A metronome used to be a stand-alone machine, but today it is a readily-available app.

TEMPO		
Italian	Definition	BPM
Largo	Very slowly	♩ = 40-60
Adagio	Slowly	♩ = 60-80
Andante	Walking pace	♩ = 80-108
Moderato	Moderate	♩ = 108-120
Allegro	Fast	♩ = 120-156
Vivace	Very fast	♩ = 156-176
Presto	Very, very fast	♩ = 176 and up
TEMPO CHANGES		
Ritardando (rit.) = Gradually slow down		
Accelerando (accel.) = Gradually speed up		

The songs in this book can be played at any tempo, particularly when you are in the learning stages. The indicated tempo will give you a goal, and is especially helpful if you aren't familiar with a tune by its title.

LOVE ME TENDER
Words and Music by ELVIS PRESLEY and VERA MATSON

DANGER ZONE
from the Motion Picture TOP GUN
Words and Music by GIORGIO MORODER and TOM WHITLOCK

TIE (review): the last note begins on an upbeat: "Dan - ger   zone" _
                                             1   2   & ___

REMINDER: KEY SIGNATURE

Always look at the key signature before playing.

This song is in the key of G Major (Concert B♭) and has one sharp (F#) which uses the right hand middle finger. Is "Hush Little Baby" in this key also?

THE LONGEST TIME
Words and Music by BILLY JOEL

HUSH, LITTLE BABY
Carolina Folk Lullaby

SWEET DREAMS ARE MADE OF THESE
Words and Music by ANNIE LENNOX and DAVID STEWART

THE GODFATHER (LOVE THEME)
by NINO ROTA

Moderato

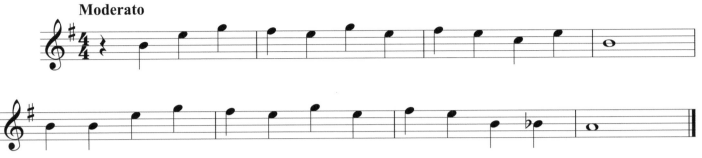

ROCK AND ROLL ALL NITE
Words and Music by PAUL STANLEY and GENE SIMMONS

Allegro

THE SIAMESE CAT SONG
from THE LADY AND THE TRAMP
Words and Music by SONNY BURKE and PEGGY LEE

Moderato

TO A WILD ROSE
By EDWARD MACDOWELL

Andante

PICKUP NOTES

Brahms Symphony No. 1 appears to have one beat in the first measrue. This is a **pickup note**, and comes before the first measure. Notice that the final measure has only three beats despite the 4/4 time signature. This justifies the single beat at the beginning.

Pickup notes are not always justified by the final measure, but will be throughout this book.

SYMPHONY NO. 1 IN C MINOR
4th Movement Excerpt
By Johannes Brahms

REMINDER: REED STORAGE

Always store your reed properly or it may not work well the next time. Never leave it on the mouthpiece when stored.

The fragile tip of the reed is susceptible to damage, and the organic material can change due to the environment. See the Sax Talk article on page 121 for more information.

JUPITER
from THE PLANETS
By GUSTAV HOLST

GOIN' OUT OF MY HEAD
Words and Music by TEDDY RANDAZZO and BOBBY WEINSTEIN

Moderato

SHE'LL BE COMING 'ROUND THE MOUNTAIN
Traditional

Allegro

NA NA HEY HEY KISS HIM GOODBYE
Words and Music by GARY DE CARLO, DALE FRASHUER and PAUL LEKA

Allegro

RONDEAU

By JEAN JOSEPH MOURET

Moderato

> **TOOLBOX**
>
> **DOTTED RHYTHMS**
>
> A dot adds half of a note's value to itself.
>
> 𝅗𝅥. = 𝅗𝅥 + ♩ = 3 beats *(Home on the Range)*   = ♩ + ♪ = 1-1/2 beats *(London Bridge* on page 30.)

HOME ON THE RANGE

Traditional

Moderato

LONDON BRIDGE

Traditional

ODE TO JOY

from SYMPHONY NO. 9 IN D MINOR, FOURTH MOVEMENT CHORAL THEME

Words by Henry van Dyke · Music by Ludwig van Beethoven

Moderato

> **TOOLBOX**
>
> ### NOTE NAMES
>
> If you don't have all the note names memorized, the solution is straightforward.
>
> Continually quiz yourself as you play the songs. For example, think to yourself, "Let's see... this Mozart piece begins on a C."
>
> This simple mental exercise, if consistent, will lead to memorization.

EINE KLEINE NACHTMUSIK ("SERENADE")

First Movement Excerpt

By Wolfgang Amadeus Mozart

Allegro

SWING LOW, SWEET CHARIOT

Traditional Spiritual

TOOLBOX

SLURS

Notes that are slurred are not tongued. Simply move your fingers while blowing. However, the first note in a slurred group *is* tongued. In this example, the first note is tongued, the second note is not.

LULLABY

By JOHANNES BRAHMS

LARGO
from SYMPHONY NO. 9 IN E MINOR, OP. 95 ("FROM THE NEW WORLD")
By ANTONÍN DVOŘÁK

TOOLBOX

REMINDER:

Always SWAB the moisture out when you're done playing to avoid damaging the key pads.

1. Drop the weighted end of the swab into the bell.

2. Turn the sax upside-down so the weighted end falls through the neck receiver.

3. Pull the swab through.

4. Do this three times.

AMERICA, THE BEAUTIFUL

Words by KATHARINE LEE BATES · Music by SAMUEL A. WARD

ANCHORS AWEIGH

Words by ALFRED HART MILES and ROYAL LOVELL · Music by CHARLES A. ZIMMERMAN
Additional Lyric by GEORGE D. LOTTMAN

*Lesson 3 review: The natural cancels the B♭ in the key signature, and lasts until the next measure. The final measure has a B♭ with no reminder.

LESSON 9:
Articulation ▶

Articulation refers to the many different ways a note can be played. It is often what gives music its character and style. Six common articulations and their symbols are shown here: unmarked notes, legato, staccato, accent, marcato, and slur.

Saxophonists achieve articulations by tonguing. The shapes above the notes represent the length and characteristic of each articulation.

REGULAR NOTES (no articulation marked)

- Lightly tongue the note and play its full value.
- There is a slight separation between notes.
- Tongue as though you are saying "tah."

LEGATO

- Play the notes smooth and connected.
- Notice there is no space between the notes.
- Tongue as though you are saying "dew."

STACCATO

- Play the notes lightly and detached.
- Notice there is more space between the notes, but maintain a light feel.
- Tongue as though you are saying "tah."

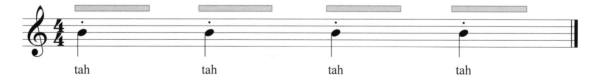

ACCENT

- Play the notes with emphasis.
- Accented notes should be stronger and longer than staccato notes.
- Tongue as though you are saying "DAH!"
- Accents can be part of a slurred passage. If so, give that note emphasis by using air, but do not separate the notes. See "U Can't Touch This" on page 37 for an example.

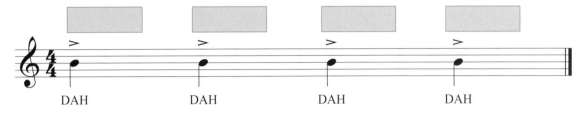

MARCATO

- Play the notes short and with emphasis.
- Marcato can be thought of as a shorter, more forceful version of an accent.
- Tongue as though you are saying "DOT!"
- In non-classical music (rock, pop, jazz, Latin) it is usually appropriate to end the note with your tongue. That is why you see the T at the end of the word (DOT).

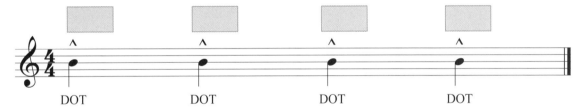

SLUR

Slurred notes are not tongued at all. You simply move your fingers while blowing. You do tongue the first note of a slurred passage. Slurs are not to be confused with ties which use the same symbol, but ties connect the same notes. Ties are a rhythmic feature and were addressed in Lesson 4.

Here is Technique Drill 1 from Lesson 6 showing different eighth note slur patterns.

KARMA CHAMELEON

Words and Music by GEORGE O'DOWD, JONATHAN MOSS,
MICHAEL CRAIG, ROY HAY and PHIL PICKETT

WE ARE FAMILY

Words and Music by NILE RODGERS and BERNARD EDWARDS

MONY, MONY

Words and Music by BOBBY BLOOM, TOMMY JAMES, RITCHIE CORDELL and BO GENTRY

WHISTLE WHILE YOU WORK

from SNOW WHITE AND THE SEVEN DWARFS

Words by LARRY MOREY · Music by FRANK CHURCHILL

BEAUTY AND THE BEAST
from BEAUTY AND THE BEAST
Music by ALAN MENKEN · Lyrics by HOWARD ASHMAN

U CAN'T TOUCH THIS
Words and Music by RICK JAMES, ALONZO MILLER and MC HAMMER

EDELWEISS
from THE SOUND OF MUSIC
Lyrics by OSCAR HAMMERSTEIN II · Music by RICHARD RODGERS

LESSON 10:
Road Maps

Examples A-E show a number of ways music is notated to repeat sections and skip to other parts of a song. Musicians refer to these as road maps because they tell you where to go in the music.

EXAMPLE A: Repeats
The end repeat (two dots) at the end of bar 5 tells you to go back to the start repeat in bar 3, then finish. The sequence is bars 1-5, 3-5. In the absence of a start repeat, repeat back to the beginning.

EXAMPLE B: Endings
The bracket with the 1 is a first ending. The bracket with a 2 is a second ending.

The sequence is bars 1-4, 2-3, 5.

EXAMPLE C: D.S. al Fine
D.S. stands for Dal Segno which is Italian for "from the sign." Fine (pronounced feen-ay) is Italian for "end." When you come to the D.S. in bar 6, it refers to the sign in measure 2. The sequence is bars 1-6, 2-4.

EXAMPLE D: D.S. al Coda
Coda translated literally means "tail" and its symbol is ⊕. In music it refers to the ending portion of music.

This differs from Example D in that you will skip to the coda instead of ending at Fine. The sequence is bars 1-5, 2-3, 6-7.

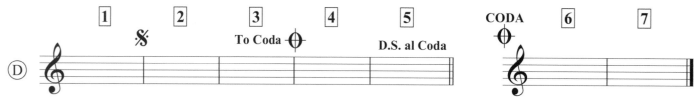

EXAMPLE E: D.C. al Fine (or Coda)
D.C. stands for Da Capo which is Italian for "from the beginning." Once you go back to the beginning, D.C. functions the same as D.S., whether to a Fine or a Coda. The sequence here is bars 1-5, 1-2.

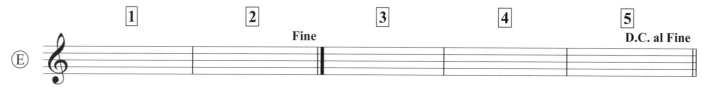

LEAN ON ME
Words and Music by BILL WITHERS

Moderato

CAN'T STOP THE FEELING!
from TROLLS
Words and Music by JUSTIN TIMBERLAKE, MAX MARTIN and SHELLBACK

Allegro

OYE COMO VA
Words and Music by TITO PUENTE

Latin Rock

BLOWIN' IN THE WIND

Words and Music by BOB DYLAN

SOME DAY MY PRINCE WILL COME
from SNOW WHITE AND THE SEVEN DWARFS
Words by Larry Morey · Music by Frank Churchill

FORREST GUMP – MAIN TITLE (FEATHER THEME)
from the Paramount Motion Picture FORREST GUMP
Music by ALAN SILVESTRI

TOOLBOX

LEGATO

When the word **legato** is marked as opposed to the symbol, it can be interpreted more generally. In this case, it is appropriate to slur notes at your discretion. The idea is to make the music very smooth.

When you play *Moon River*, treat each note as if it were marked with a legato symbol, as discussed in Lesson 9.

MOON RIVER
from the Paramount Picture BREAKFAST AT TIFFANY'S
Words by Johnny Mercer · Music by Henry Mancini

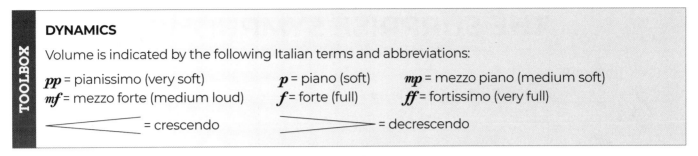

DYNAMICS

Volume is indicated by the following Italian terms and abbreviations:

pp = pianissimo (very soft)　　*p* = piano (soft)　　*mp* = mezzo piano (medium soft)

mf = mezzo forte (medium loud)　　*f* = forte (full)　　*ff* = fortissimo (very full)

⊂ = crescendo　　⊃ = decrescendo

LONDONDERRY AIR
Traditional Irish

THE SURPRISE SYMPHONY

By FRANZ JOSEPH HAYDN

Moderato

CHIM CHIM CHER-EE

from MARY POPPINS

Words and Music by RICHARD M. SHERMAN and ROBERT B. SHERMAN

Moderato

I'M A BELIEVER

Words and Music by NEIL DIAMOND

MY FAVORITE THINGS
from THE SOUND OF MUSIC
Lyrics by OSCAR HAMMERSTEIN II · Music by Richard Rodgers

THEME FROM "JURASSIC PARK"
from the Universal Motion Picture JURASSIC PARK
Composed by JOHN WILLIAMS

LESSON 11:
Syncopation

Syncopation is a rhythm in which a long or emphasized note begins in an unexpected place. The spiritual "Sometimes I Feel Like a Motherless Child" will be used to demonstrate two common syncopations.

1. In 4/4 time, the primary beats are often one and three. Syncopation can occur when a long note does not begin on a primary beat, as seen in the first measure.

Some - times   I   feel   like   a   moth - er - less   child.
1   2   (3)   4

2. Syncopation also occurs when a longer note begins on an upbeat and is held over a downbeat. Although this rhythm is half the value (twice as fast) as the previous example, it is to be played largo, or very slowly.

Some - times   I   feel   like   a   moth - er - less   child.
1   &   (2)   &   3   4   &

It is helpful to use familiar music to become acquainted with syncopated rhythms. Here are a few excerpts that reiterate the concepts taught above.

SWEET CAROLINE by Neil Diamond (full song on page 76)

In measure two, a note begins on an upbeat and is held *over* a downbeat. This song also demonstrates how a *tie* can cause a note to be held *over* a downbeat.

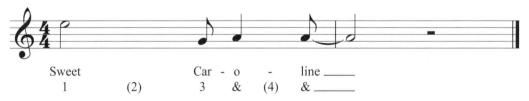

Sweet   Car - o - line _____
1   (2)   3   &   (4)   & _____

RUDOLPH THE RED NOSED REINDEER Music and Lyrics by Johnny Marks

Here again, a long note begins on an unexpected beat.

Allegro

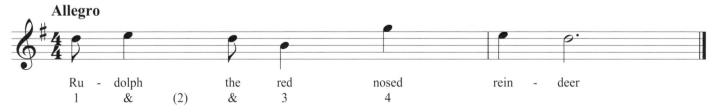

Ru - dolph   the   red   nosed   rein - deer
1   &   (2)   &   3   4

GROOVIN'
Words and Music by EDWARD BRIGATI and FELIX CAVALIERE

Moderato

CAN YOU FEEL THE LOVE TONIGHT
from THE LION KING
Music by ELTON JOHN · Lyrics by TIM RICE

Andante

BEER BARREL POLKA (ROLL OUT THE BARREL)
Based on the European success "Skoda Lasky"*
By LEW BROWN, WLADIMIR A. TIMM, JAROMIR VEJVODA and VASEK ZEMAN

Allegro

LIVIN' ON A PRAYER

Words and Music by Jon Bon Jovi, DESMOND CHILD and RICHIE SAMBORA

OH, PRETTY WOMAN

Words and Music by ROY ORBISON and BILL DEES

OLD TIME ROCK & ROLL

Words and Music by GEORGE JACKSON and THOMAS E. JONES III

EVERY BREATH YOU TAKE

By STING

EIGHT DAYS A WEEK

Words and Music by JOHN LENNON and PAUL McCARTNEY

EIGHTH NOTE TRIPLET

A triplet is a set of three notes spread evenly over a certain number of beats, notated with the number 3. In this case, three eighth notes fit evenly in one beat.

A good way to understand how it is played is to say the word itself in three syllables: "trip-a-let."

ADDAMS FAMILY THEME
Theme from the TV Show and Movie
Music and Lyrics by VIC MIZZY

SPONGEBOB SQUAREPANTS THEME SONG
from SPONGEBOB SQUAREPANTS
Words and Music by MARK HARRISON, BLAISE SMITH, STEVE HILLENBURG and DEREK DRYMON

QUARTER NOTE TRIPLET

This triplet spreads three quarter notes evenly over two beats. A good way to learn and understand this rhythm is with familiar songs as you see on this page.

SEVEN NATION ARMY

Words and Music by JACK WHITE

CHARIOTS OF FIRE

from the Feature Film CHARIOTS OF FIRE

By VANGELIS

JUST MY IMAGINATION (RUNNING AWAY WITH ME)

Words and Music by NORMAN WHITFIELD and BARRETT STRONG

CAN'T HELP FALLING IN LOVE

Words and Music by GEORGE DAVID WEISS, HUGO PERETTI and LUIGI CREATORE

Moderato

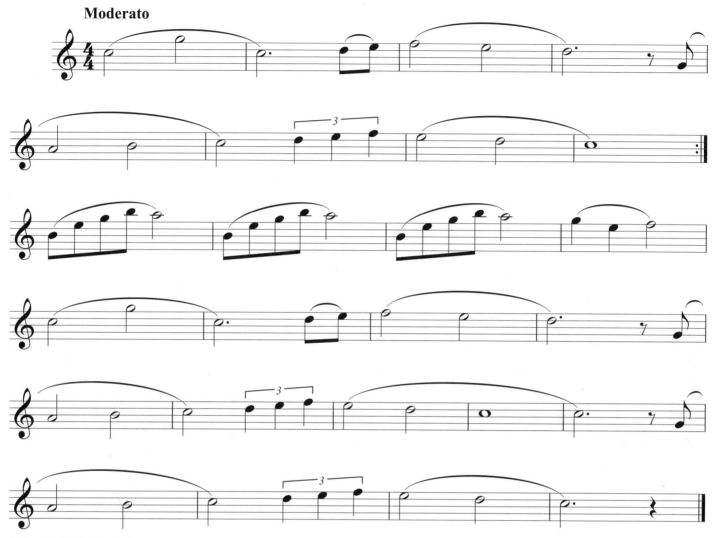

TAKE ME OUT TO THE BALL GAME

Words by JACK NORWORTH · Music by ALBERT VON TILZER

Moderato

*E# is the same as F♮.
See Lesson 17 on p.94.*

SUMMERTIME

from PORGY AND BESS®

Music and Lyrics by GEORGE GERSHWIN, DUBOSE and DOROTHY HEYWARD and IRA GERSHWIN

Medium Swing

THAT'S AMORÉ (THAT'S LOVE)

from the Paramount Picture THE CADDY

Words by Jack Brooks · Music by Harry Warren

FOREVER YOUNG

Words and Music by ROD STEWART, KEVIN SAVIGAR, JIM CREGAN and BOB DYLAN

Moderato

TOOLBOX

CUES

Cues are small notes written to indicate another part that you don't necessarily play. Rests may be above or below these notes.

Sometimes cues offer a reference point as you count rests. Other times, as in this page, you have the option to play the part.

WONDERFUL TONIGHT

Words and Music by ERIC CLAPTON

PIANO MAN

Words and Music by BILLY JOEL

LESSON 12:
Eighth Rests and Sixteenth Notes

The importance of subdividing was highlighted in Lesson 4. Here is a closer look at eighth rests and sixteenth notes. Each example establishes the subdivision of the beat before coming to the new rhythm. The ties in the sixteenth note examples show the math behind the eighth/sixteenth combinations. In other words, each line progresses to show you how the rhythm is played.

Upcoming songs that use each rhythm are listed.

Smoke on the Water, Blister in the Sun, Oye Como Va

Another One Bites the Dust, Centerfold

Beats 3 & 4 are the same as beat 2.

All Star

Iron Man, Funeral March, The Good, The Bad And The Ugly, Centerfold

Beats 3 & 4 are the same as beat 2.

To Be With You

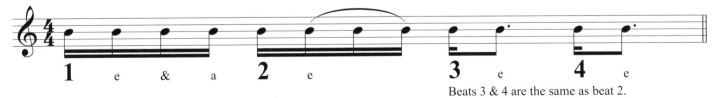

Beats 3 & 4 are the same as beat 2.

SMOKE ON THE WATER

Words and Music by RITCHIE BLACKMORE, IAN GILLAN,
ROGER GLOVER, JON LORD and IAN PAICE

BLISTER IN THE SUN

Words and Music by GORDON GANO

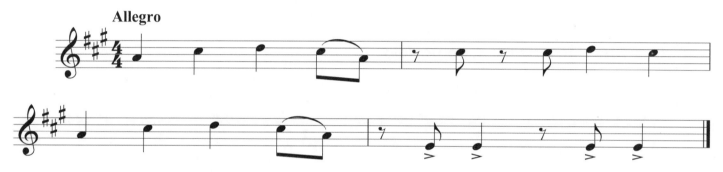

ALL ABOUT THAT BASS

Words and Music by KEVIN KADISH and MEGHAN TRAINOR

ANOTHER ONE BITES THE DUST

Words and Music by JOHN DEACON

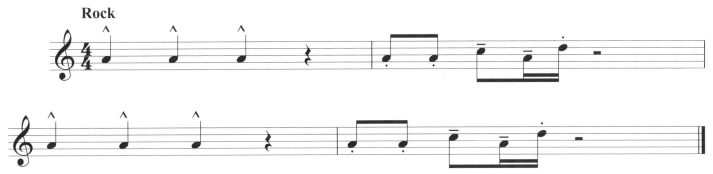

ALL STAR

Words and Music by GREG CAMP

UNDER PRESSURE

Words and Music by FREDDIE MERCURY, JOHN DEACON,
BRIAN MAY, ROGER TAYLOR and DAVID BOWIE

IRON MAN

Words and Music by FRANK IOMMI, JOHN OSBOURNE, WILLIAM WARD and TERENCE BUTLER

THE GOOD, THE BAD AND THE UGLY (MAIN TITLE)

from THE GOOD, THE BAD AND THE UGLY
By ENNIO MORRICONE

Galloping

FUNERAL MARCH

from PIANO SONATA IN B-FLAT MINOR, OP. 35
By Fryderyk Chopin

Largo

CENTERFOLD

Words and Music by SETH JUSTMAN

Moderato

TO BE WITH YOU

Words and Music by ERIC MARTIN and DAVID GRAHAME

Moderato

THE STAR-SPANGLED BANNER

Words by FRANCIS SCOTT KEY · Music by JOHN STAFFORD SMITH

SWING EIGHTH NOTES

Jazz and shuffle rock sometimes require that you swing the eighth notes. At medium tempos and slower, this means that the first of two eighth notes is slightly longer which gives it a bouncy feel.

A more precise explanation is that two eighth notes are played as the first and third notes of an eighth note triplet set.

"It You're Happy and You Know It" is a good example of swinging eighth notes.

IF YOU'RE HAPPY AND YOU KNOW IT

Words and Music by L. SMITH

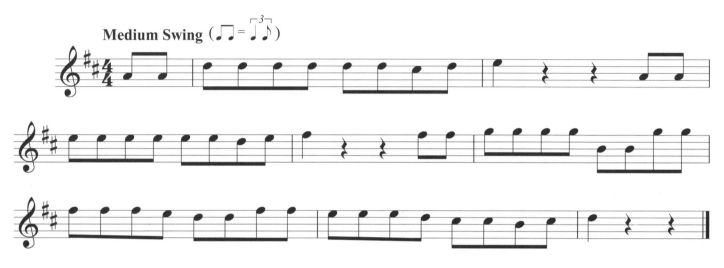

THE CANDY MAN

from WILLY WONKA AND THE CHOCOLATE FACTORY

Words and Music by LESLIE BRICUSSE and ANTHONY NEWLEY

FLY ME TO THE MOON (IN OTHER WORDS)

Words and Music by BART HOWARD

TOOLBOX

STRAIGHT EIGHTH NOTES

This song includes indication for "swing 8ths" and "straight 8ths." Straight 8ths simply means to play the 8th notes as normal, not swung.

THE BANANA BOAT SONG

Jamaican Work Song

ROLLING IN THE DEEP

Words and Music by ADELE ADKINS and PAUL EPWORTH

LESSON 13:
Intonation

Intonation refers to the accuracy of a pitch. It does not refer to whether you are playing the right note, but rather the exactness of that note.

FREQUENCY

Pitch is measured as a unit of frequency known as hertz (symbol: Hz). A hertz is one cycle of a longitudinal sound wave per second. The human ear can perceive pitch in a range from 20 Hz to 16,000 Hz. In the United States, the accepted standard for tuning and manufacturing musical instruments is A=440 Hz (second space on the staff in concert pitch, top line F♯ for alto saxophone).

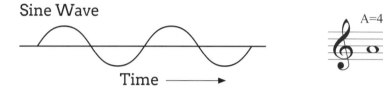

IN TUNE VS. OUT OF TUNE

When two or more instruments play the same pitch but with non-matching frequencies, those pitches clash with each other. The result is an undesirable sound, and we say that they are "out of tune". For instance, if two instruments play the aforementioned A, one at a frequency of 432 Hz and the other at a frequency of 449 Hz, they will not sound in tune. In contrast, when two or more instruments play at the same frequency it will sound as though only one instrument is playing; their pitches are a complete match.

Here's a more layman explanation of intonation:
- If two or more instruments play the same pitch and match, they are in tune and it sounds good.
- If they play the same pitch but do not quite match, they are out of tune and it does not sound good.

HOW TO TUNE THE SAXOPHONE

Tuning your saxophone is a matter of determining whether your pitch is too high (sharp) or too low (flat) and making necessary adjustments. Accomplishing this by ear is good practice and will develop your "musician ears." However, it is perfectly viable (in fact recommended) to use an electronic tuner. Tuners are readily available as an app for your smartphone or other device.

A tuner will show you whether you are sharp or flat, and is often measured in "cents." A cent is 1/100th of the smallest interval in music (a half step). This gives you an idea of how small a cent of pitch is. An example of how musicians refer to cents is "It sounds like I'm at least twenty cents flat."

1. Play an F♯ with the octave key. You can play any note with a tuner, but F♯ is a stable note for the saxophone.
2. If the tuner shows you are sharp, pull the mouthpiece out to reveal more of the neck cork. This will lengthen your instrument and lower your pitch.
3. If the tuner shows you are flat, push the mouthpiece farther on, hiding more of the neck cork. This will shorten your instrument and raise your pitch.
4. Use trial and error until the tuner shows that you are in tune.

WHAT THIS MEANS FOR YOU

When you play alone, it's tempting to think that intonation doesn't matter. However, you will do well to tune every time you practice so that when it comes time to play with others (or a recording) you'll know what to do. What's more, playing in tune requires the reinforcement of habits that are essential to playing the saxophone, namely: air support and embouchure. For further study, including things you can do every day to improve intonation, see the article "Intonation" in Sax Talk on page 124.

ISN'T SHE LOVELY

Words and Music by STEVIE WONDER

STAND BY ME

Words and Music by JERRY LEIBER, MIKE STOLLER and BEN E. KING

Moderato

LEGEND SPOTLIGHT: Charlie Parker

Charlie Parker (1920-1955) was a jazz saxophonist from Kansas City, and is considered one of the most influential musicians in modern history. He was a visionary leader in the development of bebop, a style of jazz that expanded harmonic and melodic vocabulary across many genres. His improvisational playing was virtuosic for its time. Subsequent generations of musicians to this day emulate his style as a rite of passage. Notable contemporaries include Dizzy Gillespie, Miles Davis and Thelonious Monk.

Parker is known simply as "Bird," shortened from his nickname "Yardbird." Many of his song titles are a nod to this moniker, including "Bird Gets the Worm," "Ornithology" and "Yardbird Suite."

He is synonymous with the alto saxophone you are learning to play. Online video research is encouraged in addition to learning one of his compositions: *Now's the Time.* This song uses the 12-bar blues form which will be covered in Lesson 18.

William P. Gottlieb/Ira and Leonore S. Gershwin Fund Collection, Music Division, Library of Congress

NEW NOTE: G♯

NOW'S THE TIME
By CHARLIE PARKER

SWEET CAROLINE

By NEIL DIAMOND

YESTERDAY

Words and Music by JOHN LENNON and PAUL McCARTNEY

LESSON 14:
Intervals

Musicians develop the ability to recognize intervals (the distance between notes) by ear and by sight. An interval is measured by counting the lower note as one. We'll start here with intervals found in the G Major Scale.

Intervals are referred to as "first, second" rather than "one, two", etc. The M stands for Major and the P stands for Perfect. For the purpose of this lesson, it will suffice to know that M distinguishes an interval from its minor (m), diminished, and augmented counterparts – which will not be covered here.

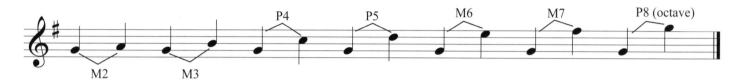

The following examples feature intervals from the major scale in a song. This is very useful when you need to identify an interval that you are hearing. For instance, if you aren't sure if an interval is a fourth or a fifth, match it against the examples below.

M2: Happy Birthday

P5: Twinkle, Twinkle Little Star

M3: When the Saints Go Marching In

M6: Hush, Little Baby

P4: Here Comes the Bride

M7: Take On Me

P4: Amazing Grace

P8 (octave): Over the Rainbow

MERCY, MERCY, MERCY

By Josef Zawinul

HAVE I TOLD YOU LATELY

Words and Music by VAN MORRISON

CUPID SHUFFLE

Words and Music by BRYSON BERNARD

EYE OF THE TIGER
Theme from ROCKY III
Words and Music by FRANK SULLIVAN and JIM PETERIK

Y.M.C.A.

Words and Music by JACQUES MORALI, HENRI BELOLO and VICTOR WILLIS

HEY YA!

Words and Music by ANDRE BENJAMIN

LESSON 15:
Cut Time

Cut time is a time signature of 2/2. There are two beats in each measure and the half note receives one beat. Because the quarter note normally receives the beat, cut time can be thought of as double the speed of 4/4 time. Just as 4/4 is sometimes labeled **C** (common time), cut time is sometimes labeled **¢** (cut time). The purpose of cut time is to give the feeling of two pulses in each measure.

Songs on this page and the page following are written first in common time, then cut time. Both versions will sound the exactly the same when played with the same pulse; the listener will not know if you are in 4/4 or cut time. There will be four beats in each measure of 4/4, and only two beats in 2/2 time.

MUSETTE
By JOHANN SEBASTIAN BACH

Four Beats Each Measure:

Two Beats Each Measure:

SUPERCALIFRAGILISTICEXPIALIDOCIOUS

from MARY POPPINS

Words and Music by RICHARD M. SHERMAN and ROBERT B. SHERMAN

Four Beats Each Measure:

Two Beats Each Measure:

YOU CAN'T HURRY LOVE

Words and Music by EDWARD HOLLAND JR., LAMONT DOZIER and BRIAN HOLLAND

Allegro, ♩ = 92

Reminder: this is the symbol for cut time,
and is the same as 2/2 on the previous pages.

The lyrics to the next song are included and may help you with the rhythms in cut time. Remember that cut time is displayed as either 𝄵 or 2/2.

(SITTIN' ON) THE DOCK OF THE BAY
Words and Music by STEVE CROPPER and OTIS REDDING

Moderato

Sit - tin' in the morn - ing sun, _____ I'll be
Watch - in' _____ the ships _____ roll in. _____ Then I'll

sit - tin' when the eve - ning comes. _____
watch 'em roll a - way _____ a - gain. _____

Sit - tin' on the dock of the bay, _____ watch - ing the tide _____

roll _____ a - way. _____ Sit - tin' on the

dock of the bay, _____ wast - in' time. _____

LESSON 16:
6/8 Time

6/8 TIME

In 6/8 time there are six beats in each measure and the eighth note is worth one beat. Beats one and four are the strong beats. This time signature has a swinging, loping feel. If you can skip to it, it is likely in 6/8.

IN 6 (slower)

There are two ways to count in 6/8 depending on the tempo. If the music is slow, count all six eighth notes "1-2-3-4-5-6". This is called playing "in six." This is the preferred way to count "We Are the Champions" on page 91.

IN TWO (faster)

If the music is fast, there are two main pulses rather than six. It is a bit cumbersome to count the numbers at this tempo, so the eighth notes are counted "1-&-a-2-&-a." This is called playing "in two." A good way to remember how "in two" sounds and feels is to say "nah-nah-a-boo-boo" which is shown at the bottom of this page. In faster 6/8 time (in two), the dotted quarter note gets one beat.

Below are some common rhythm patterns you will find in 6/8. Both methods of counting are provided here and in the first three songs in this lesson. The large bold letters indicate the two strong beats in each measure. Arrows indicate strong beats when there are no notes there (ties and rests).

Say, clap and play:

89

POP GOES THE WEASEL

Traditional

THE MULBERRY BUSH

Traditional

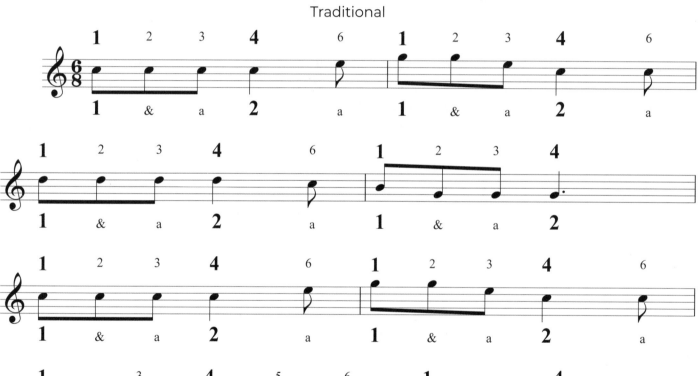

WE ARE THE CHAMPIONS
Words and Music by Freddie Mercury

I'M POPEYE THE SAILOR MAN
Theme from the Paramount Cartoon POPEYE THE SAILOR
Words and Music by Sammy Lerner

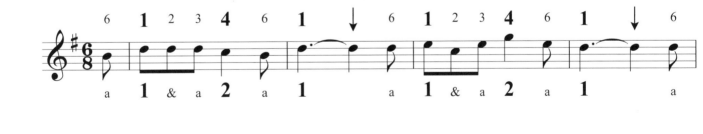

HALLELUJAH

Words and Music by Leonard Cohen

12/8

In 12/8 time there are 12 beats per measure and each eighth note receives one beat. It is often counted in four: "1-&-a, 2-&-a, 3-&-a, 4-&-a." When in four, the dotted quarter note receives one beat.

See lesson 16 (6/8 time) for further study.

TOOLBOX

BELIEVER

Words and Music by DAN REYNOLDS, WAYNE SERMON, BEN MCKEE, DANIEL PLATZMAN,
JUSTIN TRANTOR, MATTIAS LARSSON and ROBIN FREDRICKSSON

LESSON 17:
Chromatics and Enharmonics

REVIEW (LESSON 3)

A half-step is the smallest interval (distance) between two notes. A note is altered by one-half step the following three ways:

♭ FLAT
Lowers a note
one half step

♯ SHARP
Raises a note
one half step

♮ NATURAL
Cancels a
sharp or flat

CHROMATIC

Chromatic generally refers to notes outside of a given key signature, which are displayed using the above symbols. The word chromatic comes from the Greek khrōmatikos which means "relating to color." We use the word outside of music to mean very colorful, or having a sensation of colorful phenomenon. Just as a variety of colors add visual interest, chromatic notes add interest to music.

ENHARMONIC

The piano keyboard is a useful illustration for studying notes. Music ascends in pitch from left to right, and descends in pitch from right to left. Every adjacent note is one half-step apart. Two half-steps is one whole-step.

Every pitch has two names. For instance, the black key between C and D is arrived at by either raising the C or lowering the D. The resulting C♯ and a D♭ are enharmonic to each other; they are the same note.

There are two sets of white keys that have no black key in between: E to F, and B to C. These notes are already one half-step apart and contain enharmonic spellings as well, although you won't encounter them as often: E♯ and F, F♭ and E, B♯ and C, C♭ and B. Again, these are uncommon, but you'll find an E♯ in "Take Me Out to the Ball Game" on page 57.

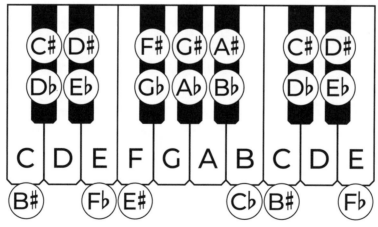

QUIZ

Here are few questions to check your understanding:

1. What note is enharmonic to an A♭?

2. What note is one half-step below E?

3. What note is one whole-step above B (remember: a whole-step is two half-steps)?

4. What note is one half-step above F♯?

CHROMATIC SCALE

A chromatic scale is made entirely of half-steps. This one-octave chromatic scale beginning on G will familiarize you with most of the fingerings on your saxophone and acquaint you with enharmonic spellings. Ascending notes are spelled with sharps and descending notes with flats. You will use the same fingerings both ways.

You have already encountered these notes in the book to this point. However, you have not yet encountered all enharmonic spellings. For example, when you see G♭ on the way down, remember that it is the same note as F♯. Use all three alternate fingerings, including the alternate C from page 18.

The chromatic scale above will enable you to learn many notes beyond the octave it encompasses thanks to the thumb (octave) key. The longer chromatic scale below has all the same fingerings with and without the thumb. To be more specific, the fingerings for the first note (low D) through the fourth line C♯ will simply be repeated with the octave key to advance all the way to the top.

This is not quite the full range of the saxophone, which requires new finger keys for the extreme low and high registers. These can be explored in the fingering chart found in the appendix on pages 127 and 128.

From D, repeat all previous notes (fingerings) with the octave key.

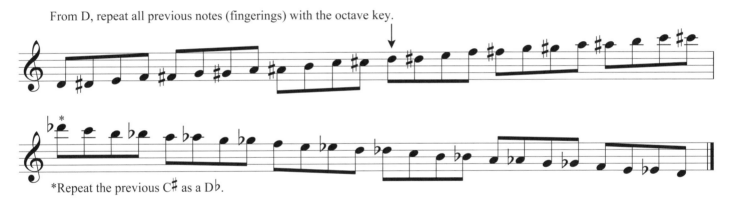

*Repeat the previous C♯ as a D♭.

"Habanera" uses a portion of the chromatic scale. Enharmonic spellings are used.

HABANERA
from CARMEN
By GEORGES BIZET

"The Pink Panther" is a song that features chromaticism. Remember to look at the key signature.

THE PINK PANTHER
From THE PINK PANTHER
By HENRY MANCINI

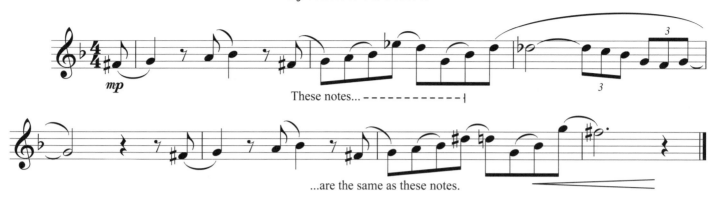

These notes... ┈┈┈┈┈┈┈

...are the same as these notes.

You may recognize "The Entrance of the Gladiators" as the "Circus Song." It is indeed a workout in enharmonic spellings and chromatic scale fingerings. If you don't feel ready for it at this time, do not be discouraged; consider it a bonus challenge. It at least provides a perfect example of the chromatic scale used in its entirety.

ENTRY OF THE GLADIATORS
By JULIUS FUCIK

chromatic scale┈┈┈┈┈┈┈┈┈┈┈┈┈ whole-step

LESSON 18:
Form

Virtually all music – certainly everything we're accustomed to hearing – has form. Form is a song's organizational format from beginning to end, and is something most people understand intuitively if not explicity. Form gives you a frame of reference as a listener, as evidenced when you anticipate a certain moment or section of a song with which you are familiar.

There are various song forms that have been used over and over by composers from Beethoven to The Beatles. Two of the most common forms found in popular music will be highlighted here: The Twelve Bar Blues and the 32-bar AABA form.

12-BAR BLUES

One of the most widely usedforms in rock, blues, and jazz is the 12-bar blues. Blues originated with African-American songs of America's Deep South in the 19th Century. Those songs were typically four-bar phrases sung three times, which is a simplified explanation of how our modern day twelve bar blues came about.

The twelve bar blues has two key moments that listeners are familiar with: the chord changes that occur in measures 5 and 9. It isn't necessary to understand chords and harmony to sense these changes, which are labeled in the four blues song that accompany this lesson. Examples of 12-bar blues are found on pages 98 and 99.

32-BAR AABA FORM

Another common song form is the 32-bar AABA form which came to prominence in early 20th Century America, particularly in film and Broadway musicals. It accounts for many songs in what is known as the "Great American Songbook." This is not an actual book, but rather a label given to encompass the compendium of classic American tunes.

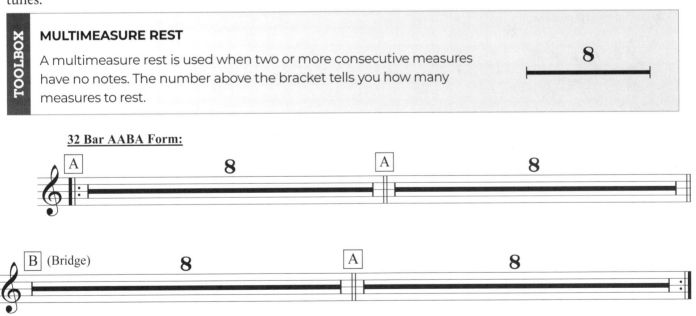

TOOLBOX

MULTIMEASURE REST

A multimeasure rest is used when two or more consecutive measures have no notes. The number above the bracket tells you how many measures to rest.

32 Bar AABA Form:

The form is made up entirely of two eight-bar sections labeled A and B. The A section is stated and repeated, then the B section is played before one final A section: thus AABA.

The B section is nicknamed the "bridge," due to both the letter B and the fact that it serves as a bridge between the beginning and end of a song. Musicians are known to point to the bridge of their nose as a signal to fellow musicians that the B section is approaching.

The casual listener understands the bridge as the part of a song that's different than the rest. For this reason, a bridge can also be generalized to mean just that: a part of a song that is a shift, or departure from the main body of the song's form, whether or not it's an AABA Form. A good example from of a song with a bridge is *Uptown Girl* by Billy Joel on page 106.

There are three songs in AABA form that accompany this lesson on pages 100-102. Each section is labeled.

12-BAR BLUES

HOUND DOG
Words and Music by JERRY LEIBER and MIKE STOLLER

12-BAR BLUES

THE TWIST
Words and Music by HANK BALLARD

NEW NOTE: B♭ (bis B♭)

This little key is called bis B♭. The index finger is used to press both keys at once. This is one of the several ways to finger B♭, and this is the one suitable for "Rock Around the Clock."

12-BAR BLUES

ROCK AROUND THE CLOCK
Words and Music by MAX C. FREEDMAN and JIMMY DeKNIGHT

NEW NOTE: B♭ (bis B♭)

This is also bis B♭, one octave above the new note in "Rock Around the Clock."

12-BAR BLUES

SWEET HOME CHICAGO
Words and Music by ROBERT JOHNSON

BREATH MARK 𝄒

A **breath mark** indicates where you should breathe, and tells you just as much about where *not* to breathe. This speaks to the idea of *phrasing*. Just as you come to a comma in a sentence, music has a natural flow that determines when you breathe.

32-BAR AABA FORM

OVER THE RAINBOW
from THE WIZARD OF OZ
Music by HAROLD ARLEN · Lyric by E.Y. "YIP" HARBURG

32-BAR AABA FORM

MISTY

Words by JOHNNY BURKE · Music by ERROLL GARNER

WHAT A WONDERFUL WORLD

Words and Music by GEORGE DAVID WEISS and BOB THIELE

In this lesson we learned about two song forms: the 12-bar blues and the 32-bar AABA form. "Can't Buy Me Love" by the Beatles is a unique combination of the two. It is an AABA song where the A section is a 12-bar blues. This makes it longer than the typical AABA song where all sections are eight bars long. The form, then is:

A. 12-Bar Blues

A. 12-Bar Blues

B. Bridge

A. 12-Bar Blues

BLUES WITH A BRIDGE

CAN'T BUY ME LOVE

Words and Music by JOHN LENNON and PAUL McCARTNEY

LESSON 19:
Other Keys

So far you have encountered four out of twelve possible key signatures. Learning all twelve keys and their major scales is a given for the serious musician, and generally takes several years of study to master. If you take on the key signatures and scales in this book, you are in fantastic shape.

Two songs from earlier in the book are reintroduced here in a few new keys: "Livin' On a Prayer" and "Lean On Me." The first key is the same as the key in those pages. An explanation of the concert pitch in parentheses can be found in Lesson 7.

In these short examples, identify the sharps or flats in the key signature, then find them in the song. Your familiarity with the song will allow you to check yourself; if you hear a wrong note, it is likely a note affected by the key signature.

LEAN ON ME
Words and Music by BILL WITHERS

1a: In the Key of C (Concert E♭); no sharps or flats

1b: In the Key of E (Concert G); 4 sharps: F♯, C♯, G♯ & D♯

1c: In the Key of B♭ (Concert D♭); 2 flats: B♭ & E♭

LIVIN' ON A PRAYER

Words and Music by JON BON JOVI, DESMOND CHILD and RICHIE SAMBORA

2a: In the Key of C (Concert E♭); no sharps or flats

2b: In the Key of E (Concert G); 4 sharps: F♯, C♯, G♯ & D♯

2c: In the Key of B (Concert D); 5 sharps: F♯, C♯, G♯, D♯ & A♯*

2d: In the Key of B♭ (Concert D♭); 2 flats: B♭ & E♭

2e: In the Key of E♭ (Concert G♭); 3 flats: B♭, E♭ & A♭**

***NEW NOTE: A♯** *(Same as B♭)*

****NEW NOTE: A♭**

MODULATION

A **modulation** is a key signature change during a song.

"Uptown Girl" has three key signatures. It begins in the Key of G (Concert B♭) with one sharp, and in bar 21 changes to the key of E♭ (Concert G♭) with three flats. It returns to the key of G at the 𝄋 in bar five. It then changes at the coda to the key of B♭ (Concert D♭) with two flats before returning to the key of G for the ending.

Courtesy flats, sharps and naturals are sometimes provided in parentheses the first time those notes are affected by a key change.

On the next page, there are opportunities to use two different fingerings for B♭: the side B♭ shown on page 21 and the bis B♭ shown on page 99.

UPTOWN GIRL
Words and Music by BILLY JOEL

*bis B♭   *side B♭
(page 99)   (page 21)

NEW NOTE: D (*palm key*)

DIVISI and OPTIONAL

When two or more notes are stacked together, you may see either "div." (divisi) or "opt." (optional).
Divisi is Italian for *divided*, and only applies when playing with other musicians.

Optional means that you choose which note to play based on the situation. In this case, you can choose between the upper and lower notes based on your comfort level with the new palm key D.

"The Way You Look Tonight," featured in the 1936 film "Swing Star" starring Fred Astaire, is part of the Great American Songbook (see Lesson 18). It changes at the bridge to the key of E♭ (Concert G♭) with three flats, then returns to the starting key of C (Concert E♭) with no sharps or flats. Courtesy reminders are provided.

THE WAY YOU LOOK TONIGHT

Words by DOROTHY FIELDS · Music by JEROME KERN

"Sherry" begins in the key of G (Concert B♭) and changes to the key of B (Concert D) in measure 21. The song returns to the key of G at the sign (D.S. al Fine). There are courtesy sharps the first time each note occurs in the key of B.

SHERRY
Words and Music by BOB GAUDIO

"Can Can" begins in the key of G (Concert B♭) and changes to the key of F (Concert A♭) in measure 25. There is no courtesy flat for the first B♭ in the F major section.

CAN CAN 🔊
from ORPHEUS IN THE UNDERWORLD
By JACQUES OFFENBACH

Previous pages focused on new key signatures as well as key changes within a song. "It's the Hard-Knock Life" is an example of a song that has so many key changes that it is preferred to use accidentals rather than a new key signature each time. This begins in measure 11 when the style changes from swing eighth notes to straight eighth notes.

IT'S THE HARD-KNOCK LIFE
from the Musical Production ANNIE
Lyric by MARTIN CHARNIN · Music by CHARLES STROUSE

opt. (see Toolbox on page 107)

straight 8ths (see Toolbox on page 70)

opt.

LESSON 20:
Improvisation

Nearly every time you speak you are improvising. What you say is not memorized ahead of time, nor are you reading from cue cards. This spontaneous orchestration of vocabulary and grammar is a marvel, yet we easily take it for granted.

Music improvisation is very much the same way. Just as we know how to say the right words in the right order, we learn which notes can be used in different situations. In this way we are able create our own music on the spot.

This an enjoyable and rewarding way to make music. However, some people may have misgivings about their ability to improvise if they don't consider themselves to be creative. This lesson provides a sure path to improvisation for any learner.

PLAYING BY EAR

Before improvising you need to be acquainted with the idea of playing without reading notes. Below is "Twinkle, Twinkle, Little Star." Play the entire song by completing each missing phrase. If necessary, take the time to stop and work it out. Consider playing the entire song without looking.

TOOLBOX

SLASH NOTATION

Slash notation is an intentionally vague marking. It allows the musician to play whatever is call for or desired.

It often indicates an accompaniment part of an improvised solo.

Twinkle, Twinkle, Little Star

IMPROVISATION

The exercises on the next page are set up so you can have fun exploring the world of improvisation. You can use any note from the provided A minor pentatonic scale. The solo lines can be played to give you ideas for improvisation. Each line displays an Am7 chord symbol which is the symbol for an A minor seventh chord. Because this book does not address chords in detail, it will be enough for you to know that the notes provided match the chord.

Here are some more suggestions that will help when improvising for the first time:

- Improvise using just one note. This is a good way to focus on rhythm.

- Choose just two or three notes. After some time, add another note, then another, and so on. In fact, the sample solos on the next page follow this progression.

- Play long notes and utilize rests. There is no obligation to play fast and fancy. In fact, "less is more" is often true in music, including improvisation.

- When the sample solos are over (in the accompaniment track), go back to them. You can play them again, or change something about them. If you change the solo, however slight, that is improvisation.

HOW TO USE THE ACCOMPANIMENT TRACK

To access the accompaniment track, visit www.halleonard.com/mylibrary and enter the 16-digit code found on page 1.

Here's how the accompaniment track is laid out:

1. After a two-measure count-off, play Solo 1 followed by four measures of your own improvisation using those same three notes. If you find you are unable to count four measures while improvising, that's alright. Simply improvise for a short while.

2. Then play Solo 2 followed by four measures (or similar) of your own improvisation using the same four notes.

3. Then play Solo 3 followed by four measures (or similar) of your own improvisation using the same five notes.

4. Then play Solo 4 followed by four measures (or similar) of your own improvisation using any note from the A minor pentatonic scale.

5. The backing track will continue as a loop after Solo 4. Continue improvising using as many or as few notes as you'd like. You may consider revisiting any of the previous solo lines for ideas.

You will find these steps helpful if you've never improvised before. If, on the other hand, you feel comfortable improvising, you can certainly skip the solo lines and dive right into improvisation. This is also an option after you've tried the steps and gained some experience.

ADVANCED TECHNIQUES

VIBRATO

Vibrato (vib.) is the repeated bending of a pitch. You are probably familiar with singers' frequent use of it, especially on longer notes. The saxophonist produces vibrato with subtleties of the tongue. Try this: with your teeth slightly apart, say "yah, yah, yah, yah, yah…" Now try it again without moving your jaw at all. As you do, notice your tongue and oral cavity (the shape of the inside of your mouth). For that matter, observe what your tongue and oral cavity do to produce all the vowel sounds, "a, e, i, o, u." It is this manipulation that produces various effects on the saxophone.

Say this series of "yah's" (no instrument). The "eee" is the elongated start of "yah" and represents the sustained pitch, as in "yah eee-yah eee-yah."

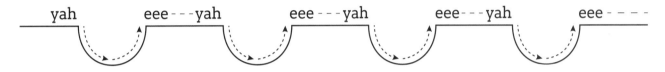

Now let's apply that effect to the saxophotne and produce vibrato:

- Play a C♯ (no fingers) and see if you can bend (lower) the pitch using "eee-yah, eee-yah" as above. It is highly recommended that you use a tuner for this exercise; it will be very evident if the pitch is bending by dropping flat. Experiment and see how low you can drop the note. Although vibrato won't typically be very wide, it's good to practice an exaggerated version.

- If you're having difficulty bending the pitch, involve the jaw by dropping it down as you say "yah." This may give you more immediate success. Then begin to experiment over time with a more subtle motion. Find a video of a professional saxophonist using vibrato; often there is no apparent jaw motion.

- Once you learn how to bend the pitch, play the following line of music using only vibrato (no tonguing). Repeated practice of this line will develop your vibrato and give you control over it, even though it's not always executed quite so rhythmically in a song.

- Now it's time to use vibrato in context. This requires some artistic interpretation which is best learned by listening to renowned saxophone players. It will also come from your own creative mind. One common approach is to add vibrato to the end of a long note as indicated in this opening phrase of "Beauty and the Beast."

Beauty and the Beast from page 37

GRACE NOTES

There is a category of notes called "ornaments" which serve to decorate other notes with fancy effects. One common ornament is the **grace note**. It is notated as a tiny note, often with a slash through the stem as shown on the right.

A grace note is very short and played immediately before the primary note. Although it's notated as an eighth note, it does not have the value of a half beat and does not change the rhythm. Grace notes are most commonly a half-step or whole step away from the primary note, although they can be any interval.

Over the Rainbow from page 100

Rolling in the Deep from page 71

See if you can find others songs in this book to add a few grace notes to. It can be a fun way to put your personal stamp on a song.

LIP BENDS

Lip bends, sometimes called "scoops", have the same basic effect as a grace note. This is done using the same technique that was covered in the vibrato section of this lesson. Because it involves motions of the tongue, oral cavity (the shape of the inside of your mouth) and sometimes jaw, the term lip bend is a bit of a misnomer.

Lip bends are notated with a small curved line before the note as seen in the example below.

Over the Rainbow from page 100

Lip bends and grace notes can be used *together* for increased effect. This could be a solution if you aren't satisfied with the amount of lip bend you can achieve at this time. Try it with any example on this page.

TRILLS

A **trill** is the rapid back-and-forth exchange between two notes, usually adjacent to one another. Trills should not have a rhythmic value such as sixteenth notes, and should be played as fast as you can. A general rule for trills is that you ascend to the next note in the key signature, unless otherwise notated. Here is an example of a trill using a song from the book.

The Banana Boat Song from page 70

Trill betwen G and A

OVERTONES

WHAT

In Lesson 13 (Intonation) we learned that pitch is a frequency measured in Hertz (Hz). The example used was A=440 Hz. There are in fact numerous frequencies present in a single note. The note we hear is the **fundamental**, and the frequencies above the note are called **overtones**. The untrained ear will not hear those separate overtones, but they are present and contributing to the quality of the fundamental pitch. It is possible, however, to produce each overtone separately while fingering the fundamental pitch.

A note's overtones are arranged in a series of intervals called the **harmonic overtone series**, shown on the next page. These intervals are present from any starting pitch, but are most evident and easily played on sax from a low Bb. The first overtone is an octave (eight notes) above the fundamental pitch, and they get closer and closer together the higher they go. Refer to Lesson 14 for a refresher on the interval names discussed in this lesson.

WHY

Practicing overtones will help you develop a professional tone (sound) on the saxophone. If you are motivated to take your tone to the next level, spend time daily on these exercises. Understand that mastery of the overtone series will take months of faithful practice. An exploratory approach to this lesson is equally applauded; try these steps and see how many notes in the overtone series you can play.

HOW

1. One easy way to produce an overtone is to play a note that requires the octave key, yet play it without the octave key. You may have experienced this phenomenon by mistake already, as often happens when learning to play low notes on the saxophone. In this exercise you will do it on purpose as follows:

   Play a fourth line D while fingering the D below the staff as shown here. You may find it helpful to "cheat" by using the octave key first. Then try to produce that same pitch without the octave key. Congratulations. You just played the first note in the harmonic overtone series, which is one octave above the fundamental note.

   First note in the harmonic overtone series, one octave above the fundamental.

   Play this overtone...

   ...while fingering this note.

2. Eventually, you will split into a note's overtones by manipulating your air and embouchure. But the steps below are another way to "trick" your saxophone into playing another overtone. This is the second note in the harmonic overtone series, which is an octave plus a perfect fifth above the fundamental note.

   Second note in overtone series: an octave plus a perfect fifth above the fundamental.

   Play this overtone...

   ...while fingering this note.

   a. Sustain the A.

   b. Quickly slap down the remaining fingers for a low D.

   c. The A will continue sounding.

   d. If it doesn't, continue trying. Use fast air and make sure all your fingers move rapidly at once.

1. Below is the harmonic overtone series for low B♭. Follow these steps:

   a. Play low B♭, which is the saxophone's lowest note. Make sure you have a good reed, take a deep breath and blow fast air. If you aren't getting the low B♭, you are likely playing an overtone; you're getting ahead!

   b. Now play the first few notes in the overtone series, one by one, while fingering a low B♭.

      › As stated earlier, playing just the first few overtones is something you can feel very good about. The entire harmonic overtone series is shown as a point of interest, and for those that may be motivated to study more deeply.

      › Play the note with its usual fingering as needed to reference a pitch to match.

      › Experiment with air speed.

      › Experiment with your oral cavity (the shape of the inside of your mouth) and your tongue position – both of which were addressed in the vibrato and lip bend portions of this lesson.

      › Try the "trick-your-sax" fingering method from the previous page. This works particularly well for top line F which is the second overtone. Sustain the F with its usual fingering and slap down the rest of your fingers all at once to the fingering for low B♭.

NEW NOTE: B♭ *(every hole is closed)*

The Harmonic Overtone Series ▶

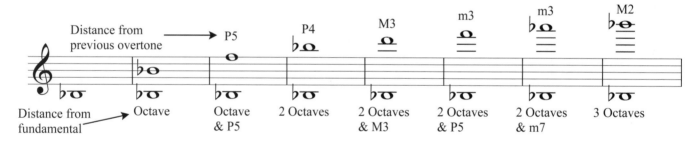

SUMMARY

It is worth reiterating that these overtones may not all be attainable at this time. Spend time exploring and sustaining the ones you can play. A recommended starting point is the first two overtones. You will strengthen your embouchure, develop your ears, and begin to hone your tone. Also, it can be fun to manipulate these notes and discover the physics involved with the saxophone.

The best way to incorporate overtones into your daily practice is to spend a few minutes sustaining each overtone for long counts (say, 10-20 seconds). Also, compare the sound of the overtone to the sound of the same pitch with its usual fingering. For example, play the top line F. Then play that F as an overtone with a low B♭ fingering. As your tone develops, you want the normally fingered note to match the tonal quality of the overtone.

Lastly, overtone study is a prerequisite for playing notes in the altissimo register, which is not covered in this book. Altissimo notes are above the highest note in the fingering chart, and are considered outside the official range of the instrument. They are a hallmark of saxophone playing in modern popular music.

NOVELTIES

The saxophone is capable of a few neat tricks. It's possible to incorporate them into songs, or just play them on their own for the fun of it.

A: THE WARBLE

- While playing an A above the staff, rapidly and randomly finger the right hand keys.

- The right hand notes will not change the A because the left hand third finger is not down. They will, however, create a unique sound. This can be an effective technique when improvising.

- Here is a possible use of the warble in a "Rolling in the Deep."

Rolling in the Deep from page 71

B: MULTIPHONICS

- The saxophone is a *monophonic* instrument, meaning it can only play one note at a time. A piano is an example of a *polyphonic* instrument that can play multiple notes at the same time. However, the saxophone is still capable of producing *multiphonics* (more than one note simultaneously).

- Thankfully there is a fingering that allows you to do this relatively easily. All it requires is that you have a good reed capable of playing low notes, and that you use a lot of air.

- Here are the steps:

  1. While sustaining low C, lift the index finger of your right hand.

  2. The result is a wild, gurgle sound. Multiple pitches are, in a manner of speaking, fighting with each other for dominance.

  3. If it doesn't happen, just continue trying. Remember to blow fast air, especially at the moment you lift the index finger.

NEW NOTE: C

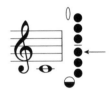

C: SIDE-KEY TRILL

Trills generally occur between adjacent notes. If, however, you trill the top side key of the right hand while playing any left hand note that uses two or fewer fingers (A through C♯), it will produce a wide trill. This can be an effective technique when improvising. Here is an example using "Sherry."

Sherry from page 110

SIDE TRILL *(with B)*

*RH trills,
LH does not move*

D: LOWER THAN LOW

NEW NOTE: A

This one falls squarely in the category of just plain goofy. The lowest note on the saxophone is B♭ below the staff. You encountered this note in the section on overtones. You can play an A one half-step below this note by inserting your left knee into the bell while playing the low B♭. You will need to twist the saxophone around while blowing.

Consider the physics at work: you are effectively lengthening the saxophone by increasing the pathway of the airflow.

SAX TALK

SAXOPHONE HISTORY

The saxophone was patented in 1846 by Belgian musician Adolphe Sax. Its early success can be attributed to the fact that it exhibited qualities of both woodwind and brass instruments. Like a woodwind instrument, it was capable of playing fast, technical music with relative ease. Like a brass instrument, it was capable of playing loudly.

Despite the early widespread acceptance of the saxophone, it did not make its way into the symphony orchestra. The orchestra's deeply established repertoire and performance history didn't have room for such a new and unique instrument. This is why the saxophone is the only common wind instrument not usually found in the orchestra today.

One can imagine how pleased Adolphe Sax would be if he could see the immense popularity of the saxophone today. It is the most prominent wind instrument in popular music.

MOUTHPIECES

Saxophone mouthpieces fall under two broad categories: classical and jazz. Classical mouthpieces have a darker tone and blend better with orchestral instruments. Jazz mouthpieces are used for all non-classical styles of music (rock, pop, etc.) and have a brighter tone.

Most mouthpieces are made of hard rubber, and their less-expensive counterparts are made out of plastic. Metal mouthpieces are yet another option, and are more common among tenor saxophone players than among alto saxophone players. However, the geometry of a mouthpiece has a far greater impact on the sound than does the material it is made out of. The most influential parts of mouthpiece geometry are the *baffle* and the *chamber*.

The baffle is the surface inside the mouthpiece directly behind the reed. The shape and thickness of the baffle determines, among other things, how much space there is between the reed and mouthpiece at the tip. In a nutshell, the closer the baffle is to the reed, the more easily it will play with a bright sound and big projection. If, however, the baffle is too close, there will be loss of control and intonation. A more open baffle will have a darker sound.

The chamber is the entrance to the cylindrical bore inside the mouthpiece, and the variance of its diameter greatly influences the tone. A chamber with a larger diameter generally has a darker sound and requires more effort to blow. A chamber with a smaller diameter has a brighter tone and will blow more easily.

As with reeds, mouthpiece choice is a highly personal matter of preference. Just as the geometry of mouthpieces differ, so does the geometry of each person's oral cavity (the shape of the inside of the mouth). If you are shopping for a mouthpiece, find a store that will let you try out numerous models. Although all the technical information in this article can be helpful, at the end of the day you will choose a mouthpiece that feels good to play. Just be sure to use a tuner when shopping so you can determine the mouthpiece's quality and accuracy.

REEDS

Reeds arguably have greater influence on your playing experience than any other piece of equipment. Ask experienced saxophonists if they would rather play a poorly made saxophone with their choice of reed, or a top-of-the line saxophone with no control over reed choice? They are likely to choose the cheap saxophone while keeping their choice of reed.

It follows, then, that it is worth your time to understand how to select and maintain reeds.

Anatomy of a Reed

Reeds are made from cane grown primarily in southern France and Spain, and more recently, Argentina.

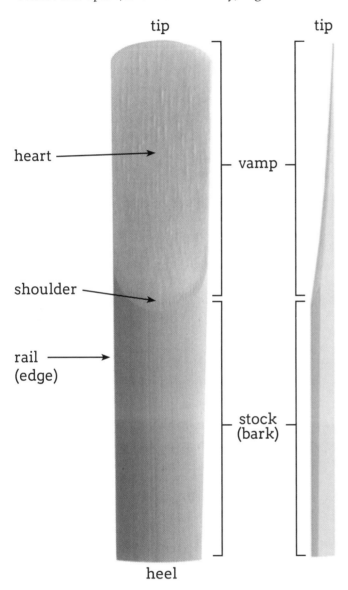

Reed Strength

Reeds come in varying thicknesses, or strength. Most brands use numbers sorted in increments of ½. The lowest number (thinnest) is usually 2, and the highest number (thickest) can be as high as 5. Other brands use non-numeric designations like soft, medium-soft, medium, medium hard and hard. Other brands combine these systems and offer a 2.5 soft as well as a 2.5 medium, etc..

What's more, reed strength is not standardized across the industry. This is one reason that reeds are, to a great extent, a matter of personal choice. A second reason that reeds are a personal choice is the fact that all people are physiologically unique. There are famous saxophonists known to favor thin reeds, while other famous saxophonists only play on thick reeds.

Despite this, there are some generalizations that can prevent you from needlessly buying too many of the wrong reed. Beginners will find success with strength 2½ reeds. It's possible the same beginner may be ready for 3 reeds by the time they purchase their second box. Alto saxophone reeds are commonly sold in boxes of ten, but some retailers sell individual reeds. Although you may spend more per reed when purchasing individually, it may save you in the long run if haven't yet settled on a reed strength.

Another consideration when choosing a reed strength may be your mouthpiece. Most alto saxophone mouthpieces are made out of hard rubber. They perform well with thicker reeds than do their less common counterpart, the metal mouthpiece. Metal mouthpieces require a thinner reed.

REED ADJUSTMENTS

Natural cane reeds are highly susceptible to changes in the environment. They also absorb water (saliva) and dry out, which further exacerbates their lack of consistency. Thankfully, there are some adjustments you can make to improve your reed's performance.

1. Tip Warping

The thin edge of the reed's tip should be a straight line. Sometimes it is warped or wavy. This is a common occurrence when reeds are not stored properly, which is addressed on the next page. Warping can still happen if the reed is stored properly, although far less often.

A solution is to press the reed onto a clean, flat surface such as a mirror, Plexiglas, or countertop. Place the reed on the surface with the flat side of the reed down. Hold the reed still with one hand and repeatedly knead (rub) the vamp section down toward the tip with the index finger or thumb of your other hand. Then check to see if the reed tip is now straight instead of wavy.

2. Tip Placement

The tip of the reed should be in line with the tip of the mouthpiece. However, this can be adjusted if necessary. If you extend the reed beyond the tip of the mouthpiece, it will cause the reed to respond like a thicker reed. For example, if you slide a strength 2 reed past the tip, it will play more like a strength 2 ½. This works in reverse. If you slide the reed below the tip of the mouthpiece, it will cause a stiff reed to respond more easily.

The reed responds dramatically to these adjustments, and you should experiment by moving it only a few millimeters at a time. This technique is handy when a reed's quality seems to change overnight. It can also come in handy if you have buyer's remorse and you wish your new box of 2 ½'s were 3's. It won't solve every reed strength problem, but is always worth a try.

3. Reed Alteration

Reeds that are too thick or uneven can be shaved. Reeds that are too thin can be trimmed. Shaving and trimming reeds is not something all saxophonists do, even among professionals. It requires skill and craftsmanship that comes through practice. If you have the temperament for this sort of work, it may be worth your while. This article will not provide a concise examination of these techniques, but rather a general overview that may prompt your own inquiry into reed alterations.

Shaving

Shaving a reed requires a reed knife which looks like a file tool. There is some debate among reed experts as to the proper method, but a few things are universally accepted:

- Never shave at or near the tip, nor the flat under side of the reed.
- Shaving is primarily done in the heart of the vamp section of the reed. If you hold the reed up to a light, you'll see the heart as the darker area where light does not pass through.
- Shave off the smallest amount you can each time, and play test as you go.

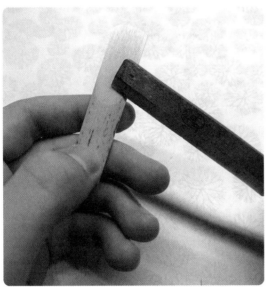 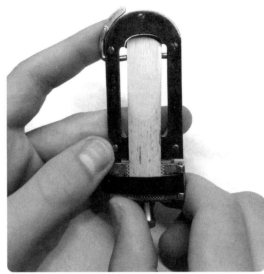

Trimming

Trimming a reed requires a specialized tool called a reed trimmer, which is designed to clip off the entire tip of the reed. Trimming has a dramatic effect on the reed, so trim only the smallest amount at a time. Always play test before trimming a second time.

REED STORAGE

Proper reed storage has everything to do with managing its tendency to react to the environment. A reed left out of a reed holder will more readily warp and change its characteristics. It is also more prone to damage.

Always wipe excess moisture off of a reed before storing. When you do store it, consider the following options:

At Minimum

Store your reeds in the individual plastic sleeves they were packaged in. Some manufacturers' sleeve design puts slight pressure on the tip which helps to prevent warping. Never leave the reed on the mouthpiece as it will be unprotected and likely get chipped.

Better

You can purchase a case that holds several reeds. These do a better job of preventing warping.

Best

Once in their cases, reeds can be given a more controlled environment using a humidifier pack. These small packs can be purchased and come in varying humidity levels (73%, 85%, etc.). All you need is one pack at a time, and they last quite a while.

The humidifier pack will allow the reed to retain its characteristics over a long period of time. It virtually eliminates the problem of finding a great reed, only to have it play poorly the next day.

This only works if the reeds and humidifier pack are stored in an airtight container. You can find one in the kitchenware aisle of a department store. It should have a rubber (or similar) seal between the lid and container. A strong sandwich bag with a locking seal will also work, but you must regularly check the seal and replace the bag as needed.

INTONATION

Lesson 13 addressed intonation and what it means to be in tune. Here we will take a closer look at this important topic, with an emphasis on factors that are unique to the saxophone.

Review

If your pitch is above center (too high), you are sharp and need to lower your pitch to be in tune. You can do this by pulling your mouthpiece out because it lengthens (lowers) your saxophone. If your pitch is below center (too low), you are flat and need to raise your pitch to be in tune. You can do this by pushing your mouthpiece further on because it shortens (raises) your saxophone. Using a tuner is the best way to assess your intonation. With experience you can also learn to tune by ear, which is helpful in real-life situations.

Intonation Tendancies

Because the saxophone is not an electronic instrument, you cannot adjust your mouthpiece and expect to be in tune throughout an entire range of notes. As you spend time with a tuner, certain tendencies will emerge that can be compensated for. The compensations suggested here are only practical when the notes are held for longer durations, such as half notes and whole notes. They are not to be bothered with when they occur as quarter notes and eighth notes in a passage of music.

Begin by tuning to the fifth line F♯, which a tuner will display as an A in concert pitch. Make the necessary mouthpiece adjustments so that you are in tune. This will be your baseline, as the F♯ is a fairly stable note on the saxophone. Now use a tuner to explore and prove the following tendencies and their solutions.

TENDENCY: Fourth line D is a very sharp note on the saxophone.

SOLUTIONS: 1. Bend the pitch with your embouchure as taught on p.116.
                  2. Add the low B spatula key to the D fingering.
                  3. Combine steps 1 and 2 if necessary.

TENDENCY: Third space C♯ is a very flat note on the saxophone.

SOLUTION: Add the top right hand side key with the side of your hand.

TENDENCY: High notes (ledger line A and above) tend to be sharp.

SOLUTIONS: 1. Bend the pitch with your embouchure. When you tune, you want these higher notes to be slightly sharp, and habituate a slight "lip bend." If you adjust your mouthpiece to tune the high notes, your low notes will be irreparably flat, as you'll see below.

        2. Use a tuner to experiment with adding either the middle or ring finger of your right hand when playing first ledger line A and above. This should not be a habit like the first solution, but could come in handy when you need to sustain a long note in a song and you suspect you are sharp.

TENDENCY: Low notes tend to be flat (second line G and below).

SOLUTIONS: 1. As stated above, do not tune the higher notes and expect the lower notes to be in tune. Instead, tune the fifth line F♯. Then maintain a consistent embouchure and avoid the trap of relaxing your jaw to play lower notes. Many players fall into this trap because their reed may be too thick, or they aren't using enough air.

        2. Reeds that are too thin can cause low notes to be flat. Review the "Tip Placement" section of the reed article; raising the tip of the reed past the mouthpiece can solve flat pitches on low notes.

Final Note

Proper intonation is a product of proper tone production, and proper tone production is the result of practicing long tones. That is why the next article is "Long Tones."

LONG TONES

When you hear a good saxophone solo on the radio or in a video, it is a distinctly professional tone (sound). Amateur musicians no doubt desire to sound that way, but may be resigned to the notion that such a tone is reserved for the world's truly gifted artists. It is encouraging to know that you can practice tone just as you practice fingerings or anything else. There is a path to a more professional sound that involves daily exercise. The key word is *daily*.

What Are Long Tones?

Practicing long tones is just what it sounds like: holding long notes. Although this requires the discipline to do something that isn't very exciting (at first), it's motivating to know what the benefits are. It's also motivating to know that it only takes several minutes each day.

It's helpful to think of tone production as an activity every bit as athletic as tennis, running, and basketball. The embouchure muscles used to produce a tone can be isolated and put into consistent, intentional use. Long tone practice is weight training for the saxophonist.

While you strengthen these muscles through consistent long tone practice, something else wonderful is happening. Your *aural concept* is also developing. You will gain an intimacy with the minutiae involved in tone production. You will begin to hear different tonal colors as you manipulate the sound with your air and oral cavity (the shape of the inside of your mouth). Even technical considerations like choosing a reed will become more intuitive.

Daily Exercises
LEVEL ONE – THE FIRST FEW WEEKS

Take a deep breath from your belly without raising your shoulders. Play each note from low B♭ to low E♭ as long as you can in one breath. When you are starting out, it doesn't matter how long you hold each note, just that you sustain it as long as you can. It may only take a minute or two to play this exercise during the first week.

Count the seconds while you play. It will give you a benchmark as your embouchure strengthens over time. It will also hold you accountable so you don't cut corners during this activity.

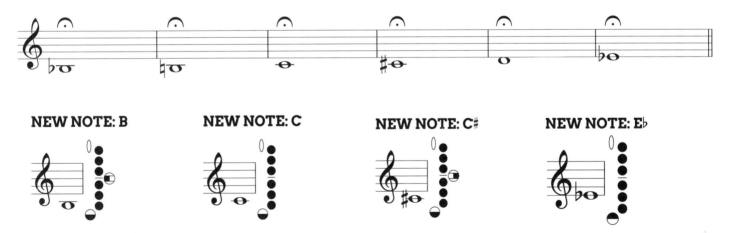

LEVEL TWO – AFTER A FEW WEEKS

Instead of playing each note once, you will now set a timer. Play each note for one minute, pausing to breathe when needed. If you don't yet have the stamina to play all six notes for one minute, reduce the amount of time to 45 or 30 seconds. Then increase to one minute after a week. After just a few days of this, you'll begin to notice an increase in embouchure strength.

Developing *Your* Sound

Long tone practice will help you develop your own voice on the saxophone – a tone quality that is uniquely yours. Another important way to develop your own sound is to listen to and imitate great saxophone players. That is why "Legacy" is the next article.

LEGACY

The art of playing the saxophone has been shaped by great saxophonists over many decades. True legends of yester-year continue to influence the sound and manner of playing for generations of aspiring saxophonists. Spend time listening to recordings of these great musicians. At the very least, you'll keep their legacy alive as you enjoy listening to their music. At most, their sound and style can be imitated as you develop your own musical identity.

In fact, the imitation of legendary saxophone players is a rite of passage for the serious musician. It is a beautiful thing that studying, imitating and assimilating those that came before is paramount in attaining the ultimate goal of the saxophonist: to find their own voice.

Jazz Giants

So who are these legends of the alto saxophone? The lineage is traced to the giants of jazz. Jazz proved to be the medium that Adolphe Sax's invention was waiting for, and it thrust the saxophone to prominence. Those musicians include: Charlie Parker, Cannonball Adderley, Sonny Stitt, Art Pepper, Paul Desmond, Phil Woods, Johnny Hodges, Ornette Coleman, and Jackie McLean.

Rhythm and Blues

When we move forward through history we find new generations of saxophonists who thrive outside the vein of mainstream jazz. Their music is distinctly different than, say, Charlie Parker. But it is worth noting that these musicians arrived at their artistic concept through a deep study of jazz giants; such is their lasting impact. These legends, some of whom are active today include David Sanborn, Maceo Parker, Grover Washington Jr., Hank Crawford, and Gerald Albright.

Jazz Today

There are many great players active today whose music is steeped in traditional jazz. Their connection to the giants of jazz is quite evident, yet they have moved the idiom forward; such is the nature of a highly creative and improvisatory art form. These players include Jim Snidero, Kenny Garrett, Miguel Zenon, Rudresh Mahanthappa, Grace Kelly, and Eric Marienthal.

The Tenor Saxophone

Legends of the tenor saxophone are so transcendent that players of all instruments have been greatly influenced by them. As an alto saxophone player, you certainly have much to gain and enjoy by listening to them. They include, in rough chronological order from the 1930s to today: Lester Young, Ben Webster, John Coltrane, Sonny Rollins, Dexter Gordon, Stan Getz, Joe Henderson, Michael Brecker, and Eric Alexander.

Transcribing

Those who wish to join this lineage of saxophone greats can transcribe their music. The word *transcribe* in this context is a misnomer, as the word literally means "to write down." However, musicians us the term more loosely to mean playing someone's music exactly as it was originally performed. Using the list above as a starting point, find someone you really enjoy, then imitate by ear something they played. Although this might seem like an impossible task, understand that the imitation of just a few notes is worthwhile. Today's proliferation of apps that slow down and loop audio make transcribing more attainable than ever.

One of the many benefits of transcribing is the ability to use the advanced techniques presented here in context. You will begin to discover and utilize the nuances of the art of the saxophone.

FINGERING CHART

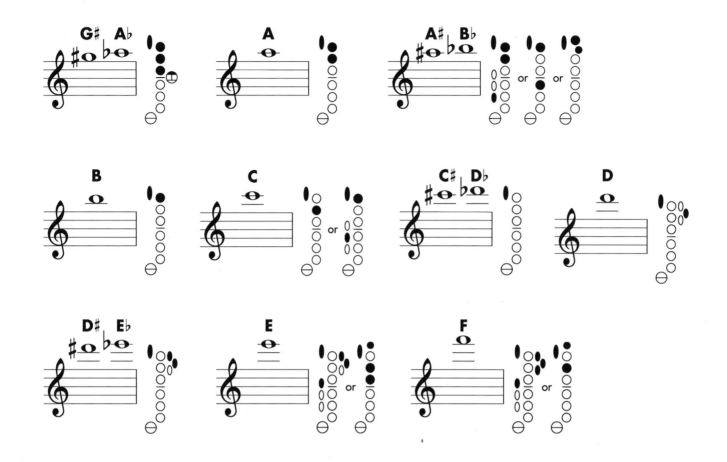